POLITICS AND PEOPLE

The Ordeal of Self-Government in America

POLITICS AND PEOPLE

The Ordeal of Self-Government in America

THE RELATION OF THE EXECUTIVE POWER TO LEGISLATION

BY

HENRY CAMPBELL BLACK

ARNO PRESS

A New York Times Company

New York — 1974

Reprint Edition 1974 by Arno Press Inc.

Reprinted from a copy in The Newark
  Public Library

POLITICS AND PEOPLE: The Ordeal
of Self-Government in America
ISBN for complete set: 0-405-05850-0
See last pages of this volume for titles.

Manufactured in the United States of America

Library of Congress Cataloging in Publication Data

Black, Henry Campbell, 1860-1927.
    The relation of the executive power to legislation.

    (Politics and people: the ordeal of self-govern-
ment in America)
    Reprint of the ed. published by Princeton Univer-
sity Press, Princeton, N. J.
    1. Executive power--United States. 2. Legisla-
tion--United States. I. Title. II. Series.
JK585.B5 1974   353.03'72   73-19130
ISBN 0-405-05855-1

THE RELATION OF THE EXECUTIVE POWER TO LEGISLATION

BY

HENRY CAMPBELL BLACK, LL.D.

EDITOR OF THE CONSTITUTIONAL REVIEW

PRINCETON UNIVERSITY PRESS
PRINCETON
LONDON: HUMPHREY MILFORD
OXFORD UNIVERSITY PRESS
1919

Copyright, 1919, by
PRINCETON UNIVERSITY PRESS
Princeton, N. J.

—

Published, 1919
Printed in the United States of America

CONTENTS

PREFACE

The framers of the Constitution of the United States and of the contemporary state constitutions firmly believed that the preservation of liberty required a careful separation and delimitation of powers between the three great branches or departments of government, and made provision accordingly. In one respect, at least, their expectations have been frustrated and their plans have gone awry. For a survey of the course of our political history and of the development of political forces and methods shows that, as between the executive authority and the legislative power, the balance originally intended to be maintained has, both in the Union and the states, been very gravely disturbed. The President of the United States has grown into a position of overmastering influence over the legislative department of the government. He presents and procures the enactment of such measures as he desires, and prevents the passage of those which he disapproves. Congress is subservient to his will; its independence is in eclipse. On the other hand, many of the state governments are working ineffectively, and the states are losing their rightful jurisdiction and influence in our federated government, chiefly because they have stripped their governors of much of the authority which their responsibility to public and political opinion properly demands.

There are those who tell us that the political philosophy of the founders of the Republic is unsuited to a twentieth-century world, that what they regarded as a self-evident truth is now seen to be only a fetish. If we are not prepared to reject the theory of the separation of powers, we should endeavor by all means to restore the lost equipoise, and to regain the ancient paths of ordered liberty under representative government. But if the new view is correct, or if it is true that executive arrogation of power is the result of forces operating irresistibly in the life of the nation, or the outcome of an evolutionary process which cannot now be reversed, then it becomes us to ask ourselves what we mean to do with our new form of government.

In this dilemma, we get but little light from the institutions of other countries. An examination of the so-called "parliamentary" or "cabinet" system shows it to be entirely unadapted to the government of a country whose constitution provides its executive with a fixed tenure of office. But the fact is patent that there has insensibly grown up around the Constitution a system of usages and conventions, which is only partially within its cognizance, and which is very largely a matter of make-believe. The question is propounded in these pages whether we cannot take this system (if indeed its continuance is inevitable) and put it where it belongs—squarely within the four corners of the Constitution. Suggestions are offered in that behalf. It is not pretended that they furnish the ideal solution of a very serious and difficult problem. But at least they would legalize that which is at best extra-constitutional, deliver the supreme law of the land from a

mocking pretense of obedience, and liberate the most
important function of a free country's government—
the making of its laws—from an atmosphere of shams
and subterfuge.

HENRY CAMPBELL BLACK.

Washington, D. C.

I

THE GROWTH OF EXECUTIVE POWER

The most portentous development in American political and constitutional history since 1865 is the change in the relations between the executive and legislative branches of government, the one making enormous gains in the direction of influence and actual power, the other suffering a corresponding decline in prestige and in its control over the processes of government. The President of the United States occupies today a position of leadership and of command over the government of the country so different from that which was intended by the framers of the Constitution that, if it were not the outcome of a natural process of evolution working through a long period of years, it would bear the stigmata of revolution, and if it had been achieved in a single presidential term, it would have been denounced as a *coup d'état.*

The men of the convention of 1787 were scrupulously anxious to separate the three great functions of government in fact as well as in theory. And hence the first article of the Constitution begins with the words "all legislative powers herein granted shall be vested in a Congress of the United States," and the second with the words "the executive power shall be vested in a President of the United States." But while they meant to keep the chief magistrate from controlling legislation and the lawmaking body from interfering with properly executive functions (except as otherwise specified in the Constitution) there can be no doubt that it was likewise their intention that the Congress should be the predominant power in the state, the guardian of the public welfare, and the ultimate repository of sovereignty. With few exceptions, even if notable ones, the statesmen of that day abhorred the idea of executive control. The personal traits and behavior of George III had no doubt much to do with this. Also the wide powers vested in some colonial governors and the tyrannical manner of their exercise had inspired them with a bitter distrust of one-man power. But more than this, their practical good sense enabled them to perceive that the mythical divinity hedging about an English king would dissolve into absurdity if applied to the officer whom they meant to place at the head of the executive department of the American system. That the titular head of the state never dies, that he can do no wrong, that his crimes against the liberties of the people, or even against one person, must be shouldered by some responsible minister, these are fictions necessary perhaps to maintain a monarchy in a free country. But the President of the United States was not to be a sovereign nor a ruler. He was to be a public agent, with considerable discretion, it is true, but only within the bounds of defined powers. Hence he was to be hedged about with law and amenable to law. And the original conception of the presidency involved a further idea, which is of special interest in this inquiry. The incumbent of that office was to be independent of congressional dictation in the carrying out of the powers and duties laid upon him by the Constitution. He was not to be the servant of Congress; but yet he was to be in large measure its agent. For the political overlordship was conceived as vested in that body which was to make the laws which the President was to execute, that body which was to create departments and offices, prescribe rules for conducting the public business, and generally, by its action or refusal to act on legislative proposals, to determine all matters of national policy.

It has been well remarked that the authors of the federal Constitution "planned a chief magistrate, nonpartisan, calm, and aloof from the throbbing political questions that might agitate the legislative branch of the government. Above the turmoil of political parties, the President was dispassionately to carry out the laws in much the same non-political manner as the Chief Justice was to head the judiciary."[1] "The makers of the Constitution," said Woodrow Wilson in 1908, "seem to have thought of the President as what the stricter Whig theorists wished the king to be: only the legal executive, the presiding and guiding authority in the application of the law and the execution of policy. His veto upon legislation was only his 'check' on Congress—was a power of restraint, not of guidance. He was empowered to prevent bad laws, but he was not to be given an opportunity to make good ones."[2] Many of the members of that convention must have shared the views of Roger Sherman, who did not hesitate to avow that "he considered the

[1] Hill, "The Federal Executive," p. 9.
[2] "Constitutional Government in the United States," p. 59.

executive magistracy as nothing more than an institution for carrying the will of the legislature into effect," and who even thought that the President "ought to be appointed by and accountable to the legislature only, which was the depository of the supreme will of the society."

Plans for the election of the President by one or both houses of the legislative body did not prevail in the convention, save as to the exceptional case when the choice might devolve upon the House of Representatives; and it may be conceded that he was finally granted a larger measure of actual power in the government of the nation than was acceptable to a group of extremists in the convention. Still it is evident that the prevailing conception of the presidential office at that time made the chief magistrate but little more than an "institution for carrying the will of the legislature into effect."   And it was thought that the powers and responsibilities of these two branches of the government, as over against each other, had been unalterably determined by the explicit language of the Constitution.

For example, the President was given a veto upon acts of legislation. But it was not absolute; it was rather suspensive and meant to force reconsideration of the bill in question; and it was ineffectual in the face of a two-thirds majority. And the opinion was long held that the veto power was intended to be exercised only in self-defense, that is, as a means of resisting encroachments by the legislature upon the prerogatives of the President, and not to make him a partner in judging the expedience, policy, or necessity of what the Congress might enact. He was made the commander in chief. But in the early view this was a military rank, not a political office; and the authority was carefully reserved to Congress to declare war, to raise and support armies and a navy, and to make the rules for the government and regulation of the forces. The President was given the power to make treaties and to appoint the non-elective officers of government. But not on his sole responsibility. The exercise of either of these executive functions was predicated upon the advice and consent of the Senate. His was the authority to receive ambassadors and other public ministers, but the contemporary view was that this was more a matter of dignity than of authority. It was made his duty to "recommend" to the Congress such measures as he should judge necessary and expedient, but no corresponding obligation rested upon the legislature to pay any heed whatever to his recommendations. The framers of the Constitution very carefully abstained from giving him any power to dissolve or prorogue a session of Congress. It is simply within his power, in case of a disagreement between the two houses as to the time of adjournment, to "adjourn them to such time as he shall think proper." Finally, and most important of all, the President has no constitutional means of getting rid of Senators or Representatives who oppose him. Should he be confronted with a hostile majority of two-thirds in both houses, he is impotent to check the course of legislation, however disastrous he may believe it to be, however contrary to the dictates of sound policy or ruinous to the best interests of the nation. In the case supposed his veto would be ineffectual and he could not dissolve the session. His only recourse would be an appeal to public opinion. But rhetoric may be persuasive, but it is not coercive; and it could have no effect until the next elections. On the other hand, a President who is believed guilty of such malfeasance in his office as may constitute a high crime or misdemeanor may be impeached by a majority vote of the House, convicted by a vote of "two-thirds of the members present" in the Senate, and removed from office.

Of course there were members of the constitutional convention and other publicists of that generation who took a different view of the presidential office, who would not subscribe to the doctrine which made the legislative branch the supreme authority in the state and the "depository of the supreme will of the society," and who claimed that any residuum of governmental power left undefined by the Constitution might be claimed for the President. They found opportunity for the expression of their opinions before the government had been five years in operation. Washington's proclamation of neutrality in 1793 was fiercely attacked as a usurpation of power belonging to Congress. Alexander Hamilton came forward in its defense, writing, under the name "Pacificus," a series of letters in the public press, in the first of which the following passages occur:

"The second article of the Constitution of the United States, section first, establishes this general proposition, that 'the executive power shall be vested in a President of the United States of America.' The same article in a

succeeding section, proceeds to delineate particular cases
of executive power. It declares, among other things,
that the President shall be commander in chief of the
army and navy of the United States and of the militia
of the several states when called into the actual service
of the United States; that he shall have power, by and
with the advice and consent of the Senate, to make
treaties; that it shall be his duty to receive ambassadors
and other public ministers, and to take care that the laws
be faithfully executed.

"It would not consist with the rules of sound construction to consider this enumeration of particular authorities as derogating from the more comprehensive
grant in the general clause, further than as it may be
coupled with express restrictions or limitations, as in
regard to the co-operation of the Senate, in the appointment of officers and the making of treaties, which are
plainly qualifications of the general executive powers of
appointing officers and making treaties. The difficulty of
a complete enumeration of all the cases of executive
authority would naturally dictate the use of general terms,
and would render it improbable that a specification of
certain particulars was designed as a substitute for those
terms when antecedently used. The different mode of
expression employed in the Constitution, in regard to
the two powers, the legislative and the executive, serves
to confirm this inference. In the article which gives the
legislative powers of the government, the expressions are
'all legislative powers herein granted shall be vested in a
Congress of the United States.' In that which grants the
executive power, the expressions are 'the executive power
shall be vested in a President of the United States.'

"The enumeration ought therefore to be considered as
intended merely to specify the principal articles implied
in the definition of executive power, leaving the rest to
flow from the general grant of that power, interpreted in
conformity with other parts of the Constitution and with
the principles of free government. The general doctrine
of our Constitution then is that the executive power of
the nation is vested in the President, subject only to the
exceptions and qualifications which are expressed in the
instrument."

Notwithstanding the severe perturbation of Jefferson and an inconclusive attempt on the part of Madison to reply to the letters of "Pacificus," Hamilton's doctrine prevailed so far as concerns the single question of the President's initiative in foreign affairs. But his general proposition—that the Constitution does not restrict the President to such executive acts as it expressly authorizes, but, on the contrary, grants him a general executive power subject only to specified limitations—soon fell into oblivion, and we hear no more of it as a matter of practical constitutional interpretation for more than a hundred years, in fact, until it was revived and vigorously asserted by President Roosevelt.

But from the foundation of the government there has been a struggle for ascendancy between the President and Congress, between the ideas of Alexander Hamilton and those of Roger Sherman. This contest has not been continuous, but it has been recurrent. It has seldom been acute, public, and conscious. It was so during the brief incumbency of Andrew Johnson. It has for the most part, however, been silent and strategic. Generally the conflict has been waged over matters of detail, that is, over the fate of some measure, plan, or policy advocated on the one side and opposed on the other. There has seldom, if ever, been manifested an avowed and deliberate purpose on either side to gain and hold an undisputed position of leadership in general and without reference to the issue of some specific controversy. And the fortunes of the contestants have varied chiefly in direct relation to two sets of circumstances. First, the matter of personal force and character, popularity, and prestige. Venerated presidents, vigorous presidents, and popular presidents have been able to impose their will upon Congress. Weak presidents have been bullied by Congress. Second, external situations, chiefly war or critical foreign relations, which have momentarily placed the President in a predominant position. A survey of American history will show the continual recrudescence of this struggle; and it will show, too, a decline in the power of the President to a point where he seemed to be almost completely subjugated by Congress and in danger of becoming little more than an executive clerk, followed by a reverse process, little short of amazing, which has led the President to a height where he stands as practically the master of Congress and the leader, if not the ruler, of the nation.

In the earliest days of the Republic those who regarded the legislative body as the supreme and predominant organ of government found themselves confronted with facts which would not square with their theories, and which postponed for a long time the eventual triumph of their ideas. The early presidents, Washington, Jefferson, Madison, and perhaps Monroe also, were men of altogether too much force of character, and with too strong a following throughout the country, to allow themselves to be placed in a subordinate position. Washington showed himself at times disposed to take a very high hand with Congress. Jefferson's plans for the expansion and development of the country did not wait upon congressional initiative, nor were they even to be restrained by his own interpretation of the Constitution. Madison could hardly

be described as a masterful man. Yet he, in common
with the others, even without the aid of specially fa-
voring circumstances, could not have failed to make
his personal influence strongly effective in the councils
of the nation. But there were circumstances, in the
first seven administrations, which did offer special and
exceptional opportunities for a strong president to
dominate those councils. Such circumstances always
arise when the relations of the country with foreign
powers become embroiled or even critical. Washington's neutrality proclamation in 1793 set a precedent
for the claim of executive control over the international
affairs of the country which other presidents were not
slow to follow. Diplomatic business, the making of
treaties, and the determination of policy towards other
states naturally belong to the executive branch of the
government, since it is that branch which must open
or receive, and conduct, negotiations. But these affairs are often of such momentous consequence, and
often the subject of such wide-spread and excited
public opinion, that the president's command over
them makes him, at least for the time being, the chief
power in the state and the nation's leader, while his
successful conduct of them will immensely exalt his
popularity and prestige. When the country engages
in war, there comes into play the almost unlimited
power of the President as commander in chief. And
moreover, in such a crisis there is imperative necessity
for the concentration of authority in a single hand.
Deliberative bodies are not fitted for the secret counsel,
quick decision, and immediate action which such exigencies demand. There is therefore always a tendency

at such times to confide much to the discretion of the
executive, and to surrender to the President the law-
making processes of the government, or at least, by
broad general enactments to vest in him every kind of
power and authority which he judges necessary for the
successful conduct of the war.

It is hence not at all difficult to account for the
strength of the executive during the early administrations (and entirely aside from the personality of the
men who filled the office), when we recall the bitter
disputes with England and the difficulty of negotiating
a more satisfactory treaty, the efforts to stem the tide
of excited but dangerous sympathy with the principles
of the French Revolution, the subsequent resentment
against the arbitrary actions of that nation, leading to
an undeclared but active little naval war with France,
the purchase of Louisiana from France and of Flori-
da from Spain, and finally the War of 1812.

Andrew Jackson, possessing the will and temper for
command, and being also a popular military hero, was
naturally bound to strive for leadership and to magnify
the authority of the presidential office.   In this he
also, like some of his predecessors, was helped by ex-
traneous circumstances.   His first administration witnessed threatening storm clouds upon the international
horizon.   Acrimonious disputes with Great Britain
concerning commercial relations with her colonies and
the northern boundary of Maine, and with France
about the payment of the spoliation claims, more than
once made war a close possibility.   In domestic affairs
his vigorous personality was often to the fore.   President Wilson aptly describes him as "an imperious man,

bred not in deliberative assemblies or quiet councils, but in the field and upon a rough frontier," and says that he "worked his own will upon affairs, with or without formal sanction of law, sustained by a clear undoubting conscience and the love of a people who had grown deeply impatient of the regime he had supplanted." Though often bitterly opposed in Congress, and sometimes defeated there, he was more than once able to bring his policies to success by sheer personal force and astuteness, the most notable instance being seen in his assault upon the Bank of the United States.

Following the second administration of Jackson there ensued a period of a quarter century during which the presidency was in eclipse. Notwithstanding the episode of the war with Mexico, there did not once occur within this stretch of time such a combination of circumstances as would enable a President to dominate Congress and lead the thought and impulse of the people, namely, the combination of a man of powerful will and initiative occupying the presidential chair with a critical situation in those affairs of the nation which primarily fall within the control of the executive. William Henry Harrison, indeed, in his inaugural address, showed a tendency to belittle the authority of his office, or at least deprecated any arbitrary or individualistic use of even the conceded and rightful powers of the President. Tyler's incapacity to fill the role of leader, even when it was offered him as a gift, was evidenced by his dealings with the various bills to incorporate a "Fiscal Bank of the United States." Such a measure having been passed by Congress and vetoed by the President, and the attempt to enact it over his veto having failed, the leaders of the Whig party asked the President to draft a bill which would be unobjectionable to him. After consulting with his Cabinet, Tyler complied with this request, and the bill which he had drawn (at least in outline) was introduced in Congress and passed by both houses. Thereupon Tyler vetoed it. The result was a storm of indignation and disgust, the resignation of all the members of the Cabinet except Daniel Webster, and an address to the people by the Whig members of Congress in which they solemnly repudiated their President. Congress at this time also, upon the occasion of another of Tyler's vetoes, felt itself strong enough to accept a report of one of its committees, to which the veto message had been referred, condemning the President's undue assumption of power.

But all this time coming events were casting their long and ominous shadows across the current of the nation's life, and at last fate brought together again a great crisis and a President strong enough to cope with it, and for that purpose to dominate all the rest of the government. Between 1861 and 1865, under the imperative necessity of war, the President actually ruled the country, and the legislative branch of government took little constructive part in the conduct of affairs, being generally content to register its assent to indispensable measures of legislation and to consider and devise the ways of raising the requisite supplies. It is only necessary to recall three measures of capital importance, all of which originated in the White House and not the Capitol. These were the first call for volunteers, the emancipation proclamation, and the suspension of the writ of habeas corpus. It is true the last was afterwards legitimized by act of Congress, but it was originally justified as a war measure within the power of the President. The Constitution may have been severely strained by the shocks of the Civil War, but it was neither abrogated nor suspended, and it emerged at the close with much less modification than might have been expected. A democracy can make successful war, and at the same time preserve its free institutions and its representative system of government—provided it lives under a constitution as wisely ordered as that of the United States, and provided it is vigilantly concerned that the liberties of the individual, placed in pledge for the common good while war rages, shall be reclaimed upon the return of peace.

Of Lincoln's successor little need be said, except that his inglorious administration witnessed a complete reversal of the division of power as between the President and Congress, and indeed showed how far the legislature can go in putting the curb upon a President, if the latter lacks the transcendent gifts of leadership and likewise the great opportunity afforded by war or national peril. Andrew Johnson's stubbornness was ineffectual in the face of the resolute will of Congress. That body assumed the command. Repeatedly it enforced its will by overriding his vetoes. It submitted the Fourteenth Amendment to the states against the President's expressed disapproval. It put through its own program of reconstruction for the South. It sought persistently to restrict the President's authority within the narrowest possible constitutional limits, as by the act which took from him the power to proclaim a general amnesty, that which virtually deprived him of the command of the army, and that which prevented him from removing appointive officers. To watch and control the executive, Congress remained in practically continuous session. Finally the House impeached the President and the Senate tried him, though the two-thirds majority necessary for a conviction could not be made to cohere.

From 1865 to 1898 no one of the successive Presidents stands forth from the background of a generally prosaic history as conspicuously a national leader, nor as exercising any remarkable influence over Congress either in the policy or the details of legislation. President Cleveland, it is true, was a man of vigor and of indomitable will; he freely exercised the power of the veto, and his views and plans often ran counter to those of the legislative body. But only twice in his career did opportune circumstance give him room to bring to the front the latent power of the presidency and elevate him to a position of commanding authority. The first occasion was the sending of federal troops to Chicago to put an end to the great railroad strike. The second was his defiance to Great Britain in the famous message to Congress concerning the Venezuelan boundary dispute. In both these crises, it must be admitted, Mr. Cleveland manifested a spirit not unworthy to be compared with that of the great Presidents of early days. And in both, his unhesitating initiative helped to vindicate the somewhat clouded greatness of the presidential office.

Nevertheless, these were but isolated illustrations of

the possibilities of executive leadership. Lacking similar occasions for the putting forth of presidential power, they made no permanent change in its effectiveness. And indeed the period about the close of Cleveland's first administration has appeared to many as the time when the influence of the executive—so far as concerns any actual control over the formulation of policies or their enactment into laws—had sunk to the very nadir. It was in 1889 that Lord Bryce, admittedly the shrewdest and best-informed of all foreign observers of the American government at work, gave this account of the matter: "The President himself, although he has been voted into office by his party, is not necessarily its leader, nor even one among its most prominent leaders. Hence he does not sway the councils and guide the policy of those members of Congress who belong to his own side. The expression of his wishes conveyed in a message has not necessarily any more ecect on Congress than an article in a prominent party newspaper. No duty lies on Congress to take up a subject to which he has called attention as needing legislation; and in fact, the suggestions which he makes, year after year, are usually neglected, even when his party has a majority in both houses, or when the subject lies outside party lines."[3] And later in the same volume it is said: "Congress, though it is no more respected or loved by the people now than it was seventy years ago, though it has developed no higher capacity for promoting the best interests of the state, has succeeded in occupying nearly all the ground which the Constitution left debatable between the President

[3] Bryce, "American Commonwealth," (1st edn.) Vol. I, p. 206.

and itself, and would, did it possess a better internal organization, be even more plainly than it now is the supreme power in the government."[4] More specifically in regard to the presidential messages, the same author observed: "The message usually discusses the leading questions of the moment, indicates mischiefs needing a remedy, and suggests the requisite legislation. But as no bills are submitted by the President, and as, even were he to submit them, no one of his ministers sits in either house to explain and defend them, the message is a shot in the air without practical result. It is rather a manifesto, or declaration of opinion and policy, than a step towards legislation. Congress is not moved; members go their own ways, and bring in their own bills."[5]

These are by no means isolated views. This opinion of the practical position of the presidency was shared not only by the statesmen but by the philosophical writers of that day. And even as much as nine years later, Mr. E. L. Godkin was perfectly justified in saying: "The President and every governor of a state have the right to send what we call 'messages' to the legislature, directing its attention to certain matters and recommending certain action, but it is very rare for these recommendations to have much effect. The messages are rhetorical performances, intended to give the public an idea of the capacity and opinions of the writers rather than to furnish a foundation for law-making."[6]

[4] Idem, Vol. I, p. 223.
[5] Idem, Vol. I, p. 53.
[6] "Unforeseen Tendencies of Democracy" (1898), p. 105.

On the general subject of the presidential office, in its actual functioning at this period of our history, we should not omit to cite the testimony of a witness who, at that time a professor in a minor college, was destined not only to become President of the United States but to exercise a more profound influence upon the relative position of the office in our system of government, and indeed upon the whole current of American affairs, than any President since Washington. In 1887, Woodrow Wilson published the first edition of his well-known work, "Congressional Government," the very title of which is significant. In that book he said: "The business of the President, occasionally great, is usually not much above routine. Most of the time it is mere administration, mere obedience of directions from the masters of policy, the standing committees. Except in so far as his power of veto constitutes him a part of the legislature, the President might, not inconveniently, be a permanent officer, the first official of a carefully graded and impartially regulated civil-service system, through whose sure series of merit-promotions the youngest clerk might rise even to the chief magistracy. He is part of the official rather than of the political machinery of the government, and his duties call rather for training than for constructive genius." And again: "The plain tendency is towards a centralization of all the greater powers of government in the hands of the federal authorities, and towards the practical confirmation of those prerogatives of supreme overlordship which Congress has been gradually arrogating to itself. The central government is constantly becoming stronger and more active, and Congress is establishing itself as the one sovereign authority in that government."[7]

Yet even at that time, those whose vision could pierce beneath the surface did not fail to see that the great powers of the presidency remained what they had always been. Though disused, they were not atrophied. The restoration of their vigor, of their predominance, but awaited the coincidence of the crisis and the man. What is more, there were those who could discern a tendency which has since become a fact. Lord Bryce said: "The weakness of Congress is the strength of the President. Though it cannot be said that his office has risen in power or dignity since 1789, there are reasons for believing that it may reach a higher point than it has occupied at any time since the Civil War. The tendency everywhere in America to concentrate power and responsibility in one man is unmistakable. There is no danger that the President should become a despot, that is, should attempt to make his will prevail against the will of the majority. But he may have a great part to play as a leader of the majority and the exponent of its will. He is in some respects better fitted both to represent and to influence public opinion than Congress is."[8]

It was again a foreign war which rescued the executive branch of the government from the secondary place into which it had fallen, and placed in its hands the attributes of initiative and command. The war with Spain, the springing into immediate prominence of the constitutional powers of the President as head

[7] Wilson, "Congressional Government" (1887), pp. 254, 316.
[8] Bryce, "American Commonwealth," Vol. II, p. 696.

of the military forces, the necessity of supporting his plans and policies, and above all, the new set of international relations which resulted, compelling the United States to take its place in the world's business as a great power among great powers, and as the guardian of far-distant peoples,—these decked the stage for the next act in the great drama. And the President was not unequal to the role for which fate had cast him. William McKinley's nature was the very antithesis of an autocratic spirit. Gentle and kindly, he had no lust for power, and sought always to gain his ends rather by the reasonable methods of persuasion than by the rude tactics of the bully. Yet in his hands, even if more by the force of circumstances than as the result of his own purpose or desire, the presidency rose again into the position of leadership and even predominance. And it was to be foreseen that it would not again lapse into obscurity. This, at any rate, was the prediction of Mr. Wilson. Two years after the eventful summer of 1898, he wrote: "It may be that the new leadership of the executive, inasmuch as it is likely to last, will have a very far-reaching effect upon our whole method of government. It may give the heads of the executive departments a new influence upon the action of Congress. It may bring about as a consequence an integration which will substitute statesmanship for government by mass meetings." "The war with Spain," he said in another place, "again changed the balance of parts. Foreign questions became leading questions again, as they had been in the first days of the government, and in them the President was of necessity leader. Our new place in the affairs of the world has since that year of transformation kept him at the front of our government, where our own thcughts and the attention of men everywhere is centered upon him."[9]

About this time two other influences commenced to operate powerfully in favor of the ascendancy of the executive. One was a doctrine of political science, the other a development of practical politics. On the one hand, it began to be argued that leadership in the business of government naturally belongs to the executive arm, not the legislative. And this for two reasons. The attitude of the legislator towards the conditions with which the laws are to deal is more or less theoretic; that of the officers who carry the laws into actual operation is always practical. The statesman in the halls of the legislature may have some prevision of the results of given legislation; but the man in the White House or the governor's chamber is every day in personal touch with actual facts, conditions, and needs. Again, whatever may be the abstract conception of government, it is the fact that the executive, not the legislature, reaps the praise or bears the blame of the administration as a whole. And responsibility cannot be—at any rate should not be—divorced from control. "Responsibility for the use of executive power inevitably implies leadership. Executive power and leadership cannot be separated. In both public and private business, those who are charged with high duties and who are made responsible for their proper discharge must be leaders or failures. On the con-

[9] Woodrow Wilson, "Constitutional Government in the United States," (1908), p. 59.

trary, irresponsible official leadership means autocracy. Irresponsible official leadership means domination by the political boss."[10]

On the other hand, the epoch of which we are speaking witnessed the revitalizing of an idea, old in practical politics, but which had fallen into decadence. This was the conception of the President as the leader of his party. There were periods, as we have seen, when the President was not necessarily the leader of his party, nor even one of its most influential members. Among the later Presidents, some have gladly accepted this office and its responsibilities; others have seen no way of escape from them. But it seems now to have become an accepted rule that the President must be regarded as the chief or head of the party which has placed him in power, and that he must, at least in all matters of a partisan character, devote his political activities (as distinguished from the routine of administration) to guiding its counsels and securing its continuance in the control of the government. Now a political party comes into power pledged to the support of certain policies and purposes which have been set forth in its platform. Moreover, the successful candidate for the presidency, in his campaign speeches, will have set forth these policies more definitely and will probably have stated more explicitly the purposes he means to pursue. The result of the election is regarded as a mandate from the people (at least from the majority), and the party assumes the reins of government with a more or less definite program, which it is the business of its elected members to enact

[10] "Municipal Research," May, 1915, p. 72.

into law   But who is to take the initiative in this?
The party probably has a majority in both houses of
Congress. If so, it has not less than 218 members in
the House of Representatives and not less than 49 in
the Senate. Among them may be several men possessing influence, initiative, and other qualities of constructive statesmanship. But the leader of the party
is the President, and thus it becomes his business to
see to it that Congress redeems the party's pledges and
enacts the party's measures. In detail, some of these
measures may be highly objectionable to individual
members of Congress. It may even happen that a
particular measure, as an entirety, is regarded with
great disfavor by nearly all of them. But it is a party
measure; there is pressure from the party leader; the
welfare of the party is at stake; and no merely personal opinions or wishes must be allowed to interfere,
nor even substantial doubts whether the measure does
not violate the Constitution.

The accession of Theodore Roosevelt to the presidency brought into play conditions which were almost
ideally adapted to work out an immense increase in
the power and domination of the executive. Much
was due to his own personality; less, but still an appreciable part, to the occurrence of circumstances
which permitted his natural qualities strongly to assert themselves. Here was a born leader of men, in-
tensely alert, energetic, courageous, and determined,
eager to make his will prevail, and glad to accept the
utmost measure of responsibility. Besides, he was
thoroughly convinced of what we have spoken of as a
concept of political science—that the office of leader-

ship in government does not suit or belong to the legislative branch, but is the natural duty and prerogative of the executive. And the practical doctrine that the chief magistrate of the state or nation is the leader of his party had no dubious sound to him. On the contrary, he constantly sought to broaden it out into the doctrine that he is the chief representative of the people as a whole, and so, not so much the leader of this or that party, as of the state or the nation. For in effect it is hardly too much to say that Roosevelt, alone among our Presidents up to that time, consistently believed that predominance in government rightfully belongs to the executive, and that it so belongs and should be exercised, not merely for the meeting of some special crisis or with reference to the enactment or repeal of some particular measure, but continuously and as a matter of fixed principle.

Actually he was not always able to translate these theories into facts. Congress was by no means submissive. The contest between the two branches of government was more than once brought out into the open and threatened to become critically serious. But if, in Roosevelt's incumbency, the new hegemony of the executive was not carved into an established fact, at least it became clear that the older notions of the President's place in the government were irretrievably gone.

In his charmingly frank autobiography Mr. Roosevelt shows us exactly the state of mind with which he approached these questions, first as Governor of New York and then as President of the United States, and the processes which he employed to make his leadership effective. "In theory," he says, "the executive has nothing to do with legislation. In practice, as things now are, the executive is or ought to be peculiarly representative of the people as a whole. As often as not the action of the executive offers the only means by which the people can get the legislation they demand and ought to have. Therefore a good executive, under the present conditions of American political life, must take a very active interest in getting the right kind of legislation, in addition to performing his executive duties with an eye single to the public welfare. More than half of my work as Governor was in the direction of getting needed and important legislation. I accomplished this only by arousing the people, and riveting their attention on what was done."[11] An excellent illustration of the exertion of executive influence upon legislation, given a strong and determined executive, is afforded by the following incident, related by Mr. Roosevelt in the same volume, which occurred while he was Governor of New York: "I had made up my mind that if I could get a show in the legislature the bill would pass, because the people had become interested and the representatives would scarcely dare to vote the wrong way. Accordingly, on April 27, 1899, I sent a special message to the Assembly, certifying that the emergency demanded the immediate passage of the bill. The machine leaders were bitterly angry, and the Speaker actually tore up the message without reading it to the Assembly. That night they were busy trying to arrange some device for the defeat of the bill, which was not difficult, as

[11] Theodore Roosevelt, "Autobiography," p. 292.

the session was about to close. At seven the next morning I was informed of what had occurred. At eight I was in the capitol at the executive chamber, and sent in another special message which opened as follows: 'I learn that the emergency message which I sent last evening to the Assembly on behalf of the Franchise Tax Bill has not been read. I therefore send hereby another message on the subject. I need not impress upon the Assembly the need of passing this bill at once.' I sent this message to the Assembly by my secretary, with an intimation that if this were not promptly read I should come up in person and read it. Then, as so often happens, the opposition collapsed, and the bill went through both houses with a rush."[12]

It was also characteristic of President Roosevelt—and a factor in the working out of the whole problem of the relation of these two branches of government—that he resisted with the utmost energy any attempt on the part of Congress to define the powers of the presidency within narrower limits than those which he conceived as its rightful bounds. On this point also we are able to cite his own testimony. In regard to his controversy with Congress over the appointment of various unsalaried commissions, he has this to say in his autobiography: "The report of the Country Life Commission was transmitted to Congress by me on February 9, 1909. In the accompanying message I asked for $25,000 to print and circulate the report and to prepare for publication the immense amount of valuable material collected by the commission but still

[12] Idem, p. 311.

unpublished. The reply made by Congress was not only a refusal to appropriate the money, but a positive prohibition against continuing the work. The Tawney amendment to the Sundry Civil Bill forbade the President to appoint any further commissions unless specifically authorized by Congress to do so. Had this prohibition been enacted earlier *and complied with,* it would have prevented the appointment of the six Roosevelt commissions. But I would not have complied with it. . . . As what was almost my last official act, I replied to Congress that if I did not believe the Tawney amendment to be unconstitutional, I would veto the Sundry Civil Bill which contained it, and that if I were remaining in office I would refuse to obey it.''[13]

But the ideas of Roosevelt as President went much further than this. He was fond of referring his conception of the duties and responsibilities of the office to the standards of Jackson and of Lincoln. But what he did, consciously or unconsciously, was to revive and apply the doctrine of Hamilton, that the Constitution contains a general grant of executive power, which is not restricted to the specific functions thereafter enumerated, but on the contrary is circumscribed only in so far as the Constitution explicitly limits it. Of course it is a necessary deduction from this theory that the President can exert his powers in any direction that is not barred by the Constitution. And this is the very core of the problem. If the President must wait upon Congress and do only what it authorizes him to do, he is subordinate to Congress save only to the

[13] Idem, p. 430.

extent to which his personal influence may prevail. If not, he is an independent agency and in many important matters may take the initiative. Mr. Roosevelt's side of the argument is thus set forth by himself:

"The most important factor in getting the right spirit in my administration, next to the insistence upon courage, honesty, and a genuine democracy of desire to serve the plain people, was my insistence upon the theory that the executive power is limited only by specific restrictions and prohibitions appearing in the Constitution or imposed by the Congress under its constitutional powers. My view was that every executive officer, and above all every executive officer in high position, was a steward of the people, bound actively and affirmatively to do all he could for the people, and not to content himself with the negative merit of keeping his talents undamaged in a napkin. I declined to adopt the view that what was imperatively necessary for the nation could not be done by the President unless he could find some specific authorization to do it. My belief was that it was not only his right but his duty to do anything that the needs of the nation demanded unless such action was forbidden by the Constitution or by the laws. Under this interpretation of executive power, I did and caused to be done many things not previously done by the President and the heads of the departments. I did not usurp power, but I did greatly broaden the use of executive power. In other words, I acted for the public welfare, I acted for the common well-being of all our people, whenever and in whatever manner was necessary, unless prevented by direct constitutional or legislative prohibition."[14]

Again, of the steps taken to settle the anthracite coal strike in 1902, Mr. Roosevelt says:

"Very much the most important action I took as regards labor had nothing to do with legislation, and represented executive action which was not required by the Constitution. It illustrated as well as anything that I

[14] Theodore Roosevelt, "Autobiography," p. 371.

did the theory which I have called the Jackson-Lincoln theory of the presidency; that is, that occasionally great national crises arise which call for immediate and vigorous executive action, and that in such cases it is the duty of the President to act upon the theory that he is the steward of the people, and that the proper attitude for him to take is that he is bound to assume that he has the legal right to do whatever the needs of the people demand, unless the Constitution or the laws explicitly forbid him to do it." ("Autobiography," p. 479.)

One further illustration will suffice to make clear both Mr. Roosevelt's conception of the presidency and its working in actual practice. He made an agreement with the governmental authorities of Santo Domingo by which the custom houses of that country were placed in the hands of American officers, and it was stipulated that 45 per cent of the revenue collected was to be turned over to the Santo Domingan government, and the remainder placed in a sinking fund in New York for the benefit of the creditors of that government. As these creditors were mostly Europeans, and two or three foreign governments were threatening concerted action to secure the payment of the claims of their nationals, this action was taken for the purpose of averting foreign intervention. Concerning this matter, he says in his "Autobiography" (p. 524):

"The Constitution did not explicitly give me the power to bring about the necessary agreement with Santo Domingo. But the Constitution did not forbid my doing what I did. I put the agreement into effect, and I continued its execution for two years before the Senate acted; and I would have continued it until the end of my term, if necessary, without any action by Congress. But it was far preferable that there should be action by Congress, so that we might be proceeding under a treaty which was the law of the land, and not merely by a direction of the chief executive which would lapse when that particular executive left office. I therefore did my best to get the Senate to ratify what I had done."

The next President brought to the office an almost diametrically opposite theory of the executive. To the conservative and well-trained legal mind of Mr. Taft the idea of a government by personal impulse, or even by the exercise of the judgment and discretion of any one man, was little short of abhorrent. In his view, it was incorrect to describe the President as the "steward of the people" or as the "guardian of the public welfare." To be sure (so he might have reasoned) the President is not in any proper sense the "servant" of the people; he is the chief magistrate of the nation, charged with very high and important duties, vested with a wide measure of discretion in their discharge, and laden with heavy responsibilities. Circumstances sometimes arise which make him the guide and leader of the people. But the orbit of his activities is always strictly marked out by the Constitution. And his every step must have the justification of law. For, fundamentally, ours is a government of law. Whatever is done must have the warrant of law. Now the law-making power of the nation is vested in Congress. True, the President may "recommend" to Congress measures which he conceives to be in the public interest and he can veto bills which appear to him to be inconducive to the public welfare. But that is as far as he can constitutionally go. What new laws are needed? What old laws should be amended or repealed? How far, within the possible limits of legis-

lative achievement as distinguished from individual
initiative or concerted individual action, is it possible
to ameliorate the condition of the general public? The
solution of these questions is for the legislative branch
of the government, not the executive. The people's
elected representatives in the houses of Congress are
their stewards and the guardians of their welfare.
That is what they are elected for.

That the foregoing expresses fairly, at least in its
essential outlines, President Taft's understanding of
our system of government and of the place of the
executive in it, may be gathered from his writings
published after he retired from office. In particular,
he has this to say:

"The true view of the executive functions is, as I conceive it, that the President can exercise no power which
cannot be fairly and reasonably traced to some specific
grant of power, or justly implied and included within
such express grant as proper and necessary to its exercise. Such specific grant must be either in the federal
Constitution or in an act of Congress passed in pursuance
thereof. There is no undefined residuum of power which
he can exercise because it seems to him to be in the public
interest. . . . My judgment is that the view ascribing an
undefined residuum of power to the President is an un-
safe doctrine, and that it might lead under emergencies
to results of an arbitrary character, doing irremediable
injustice to private rights. The mainspring of such a
view is that the executive is charged with responsibility
for the welfare of all the people in a general way, that
he is to play the part of a universal Providence and set
all things right, and that anything that in his judgment
will help the people he ought to do, unless he is expressly
forbidden to do it. The wide field of action that this
would give to the executive one can hardly limit."[15]

[15] William H. Taft, "Our Chief Magistrate," pp. 139-144.

And yet it was too late to return to any such theory of executive power as might have been entertained a generation before. Political developments had prevented that. The position and responsibility of the President as the leader of his party was no longer a proposition for debate, nor a phenomenon of occasional personal volition. It was an unshakable fact and a permanent institution. President Taft accepted it with that abundant good sense and appreciation of the practical which always characterized him, as witness his firm interference to adjust the differences between the two houses of Congress in the matter of the tariff bill in 1909 and to force the passage of an act which would in some measure redeem the promises of the party. But there is ground to believe that the theory of the presidency which had formed itself in the mind of the sound constitutional lawyer and ex-judge, William Howard Taft, was not precisely coincident with that other theory upon which President Taft, leader of the Republican party, found himself obliged at times to act. And it is perhaps fair to surmise that the reconciliation was not effected without an effort.

Mr. Taft's successor became the leader of the nation in a stupendous war. An autocratic monarch always has within his grasp the controls which operate and guide the war machine; but war is a business to which a democracy is very ill adapted. In the history of the Roman Republic it was more than once necessary to appoint a dictator in order to save the state. And any modern republic, if it would participate effectively in a war of the first magnitude, must consent to a similar concentration of power in the hands

of one man or a few men. Such a course is abnormal
for a self-governing people. But war also is utterly
abnormal. And sometimes heroic measures must be
taken to repel a gigantic danger. The specter of war
is not to be exorcised by the deliberate processes of
peace. Fortunately for us, however, this does not
mean that the Constitution is abrogated or even suspended, in so much as a single line, when the nation becomes an army. The wise foresight of its framers
contemplated even such a crisis as that through which
we have recently passed, and its ample provisions have
been found sufficient to encompass all measures essential to the country's preservation and to the efficient putting forth of its strength for the winning of
the war. For this supreme purpose the people, through
their representatives in the houses of Congress,
delegated to their President powers of such vast magnitude and range that their parallel is not to be found
in all the pages of history. For since the days of Sulla
at least, no other man has ever held, legally and by the
freewill gift of his fellow citizens, such unrestricted
control over their lives and fortunes. But he held
these extraordinary powers in trust. They were not a
part of our normal governmental life. Their deposit
was but temporary and to meet an emergency. Upon
the return of peace, the trust was accomplished and the
deposit must be restored.

The experience through which the country has been
passing, the necessary leadership of the executive as
both the master of war and the administrator of the
people's affairs, the determination by him of the measures which he judged necessary for the success of the

war, the attitude of Congress, as shown in its eventual willingness (but not without some stumbling and expostulation) to grant him whatever authority he deemed essential, the gradual habituation of the people to the regulation of their daily lives by all ranks of administrative officers—all these things must have a profound influence upon the position of the presidency in our system of government. How far that influence will extend and what will be its final result lies behind the veil of the future. And as prophecy does not fall within the scope of this study, but only history, it is only the first administration of President Wilson that can be passed under review for the purpose of examining into the growth of executive power.

That administration began with a clear field for the executive authority, since his party commanded a majority in both houses of Congress. As respects the House of Representatives at least, candor compels the admission that the results of the election reflected no great credit upon the electorate. With certain notable exceptions, the great body of the administration's followers in the lower house were much below the congressional average in respect to intelligence, experience, and capacity for the management of large affairs. In addition to this, the record of the Democratic party, up to that time, had shown it to be strong and effective in opposition, but curiously inept, when placed in power, for the carrying on of constructive work in legislation, chiefly in consequence of its inveterate tendency, when in control of the government, to break out into internecine quarrels and to dissolve into irreconcilable factions. More than ever, therefore, the

President was placed in the position of leader of his party and of the party's representatives in the Congress, and more than ever, Congress was amenable to presidential guidance and persuasion. Quite frankly the members of the legislature looked to the President to tell them what to do, and quite as frankly the President accepted the responsibility. It will not have been forgotten that his first inaugural address outlined in general terms, but with plain indications as to specific measures, the program of legislation which the party proposed to put into effect. And as an evidence of his desire for close co-operation with the legislative body, and to extend his powers of recommendation, advice, and persuasion to the utmost legitimate limits, it will be remembered that Mr. Wilson revived Washington's custom of reading his messages to the Congress assembled in joint session, instead of sending them by the hand of a secretary. About this time also it became the custom to apply the name "administration bills" to those projects of legislation which were either drafted in the executive departments or known to constitute a part of the President's program, as distinguished from measures which had their origin in committees or in the initiative of an individual member.

The country at large seemed to accept as quite natural the leadership of the White House. As a curious bit of evidence bearing on this point it will be recalled that, in the summer of 1916, when the President was endeavoring by mediation and conciliation to avert the threatened general railroad strike, the committee of railroad presidents who were in conference with him undertook to concede the demand of the employes for an eight-hour day if he would give them an absolute guaranty that he would secure from Congress legislation which would permit them to raise freight rates. No such suggestion emanated from the President. But the circumstances shows the public conception of him, then existing, as the master of Congress and the dominating figure, not in party politics but in legislation.

Substantially all the laws desired by the President in his first administration were enacted. But Congress was not completely docile. At times there were strong voices of dissent and of remonstrance against the goad. For instance, the child-labor bill was not passed through the Senate without the greatest difficulty. It was necessary for the President to hold personal conference with some of the Senators who were most determined in their opposition. Several members of that body were by no means convinced that the act, if passed, would be constitutional; but when they gave voice to their doubts, they were assured by another Senator that, in his judgment, the presidential assumption of legislative functions was a greater menace to the Constitution than the enactment of any given measure would be. Perhaps the most extreme denunciation of the tendency in this direction was that expressed by Senator Works of California in his valedictory address, delivered January 4, 1917. He is reported to have said:

"The fear of judicial usurpation of power was uppermost in the mind of Mr. Jefferson, but he and others were able to see the danger now confronting us, of the unwarranted and unconstitutional usurpation of power by the President, amounting practically to a dictatorship, and the complacent surrender of its powers and functions and abandonment of its duties and obligations by the Congress of the United States. The tendency towards centralized, unchecked, and unlimited power on the part of the President has existed for some years past, and has grown rapidly worse and more offensive in the last four years. Never in the entire history of the country has the President so completely and defiantly usurped the law-making powers of the government and dictated and forced the course of Congress, and never has the Congress been so submissive or so subservient to a power outside itself. Never in all our history have we come so near to a despotic government by a dictator as during the last four years. Members of Congress have, under the lash of executive and party domination, surrendered their conscientious convictions and voted against their own sentiments of right and justice. We have on the statute books today not one but many enactments that are the laws of a dictator and not the free and voluntary acts of the Congress, and we have men holding offices of the highest trust whose confirmation was the result of the same dictatorial power and not the free and voluntary action of this body."[16]

Dissociated from the abnormal conditions created by the war, what, then, is the present position of the presidency? The answer is that the American President, without losing anything of his constitutional authority or anything of the prestige and influence originally planned for him, has drawn to himself powers which very much resemble those of a British prime minister. The difference, of course, is that the President is not dependent upon the breath of parliamentary favor, and that no hostile majority against him, not even the defeat of his most cherished and most earn-

[16] Congressional Record, Vol. 54, part 1, p. 865; 64th Congress, 2d Session, January 5, 1917.

estly advocated measures, could force his resignation.
He assumes office charged with responsibility to enact the party's program.   But if he fails in this, the
responsibility is neither his nor the party's; it is cast
upon recalcitrant members of Congress.   The President is not forced, in any mishap whatever, to "go to
the country" in the English sense.   Mr. Wilson himself has said:

"It is becoming more and more true, as the business of
the government becomes more and more complex and
extended, that the President is becoming more and more
a political and less and less an executive officer.   His executive powers are in commission, while his political
powers more and more center and accumulate upon him
and are in their very nature personal and inalienable."[17]

The results of these developing tendencies have been
summed up, with some rhetorical exaggeration but
none the less with substantial truth, by a writer in *The
New Republic* in the following terms:

"The private individual of Congress is dead, and it is
surely important that there is none to sing his requiem.
The traditional separation of powers has broken down
for the simple reason that it results only in confounding
them.   Congress may delay presidential action; but there
is evidence enough, even apart from the fact of war, that
it is finding it increasingly difficult ultimately to thwart
it.   For congressional debate has largely ceased to influence the character of public opinion. . . . Nor is the
individual member of Congress alone in his eclipse.   The
congressional committees have become less the moulders
of legislation than the recipients who may alter its details.   Even on the committees themselves the administration now has its avowed spokesmen.   They seem to
act very much as a British minister in charge of a meas-

[17] Woodrow Wilson "Constitutional Government in the United
States" (1908), p. 66.

ure in the House of Commons. They interpret the executive will; and we have seen recalcitrant members interviewed on policy by the President himself. The key to the whole, in fact, has come to lie in the President's hands. The pathway of decision is his own, influenced above all by his personal cast of mind and by the few who can obtain direct access to him. This is not, it is clear, the government envisaged by the Constitution. Equally certain it is not a government which meets with the approval of Congress. But outside of Washington, the old suspicion of executive power is dead, and popular sentiment has become so entirely uninterested in the processes of politics as to ask only for substantial results. In such an aspect, executive action is far more valuably dramatic than the action of Congress."[18]

The fact remains, however, that certain individual members of Congress remember the ancient prestige of that body and deplore its present subservience to the executive branch. In them, perhaps, lies the best hope of deliverance from executive usurpation. A vigorous expression of this sentiment may be seen in certain remarks addressed to the House by Representative James L. Slayden of Texas, on January 15, 1919, together with a shrewd diagnosis of the situation as being due in no small measure to the subordination of principles, of individual and corporate liberty and independence, and even of respect for the Constitution itself to the exigencies of party politics. He asked:

"What is the cause of this degradation of the first-born of the Constitution? In thinking it over, I have not been able to avoid the conclusion that it is due to a voluntary surrender of constitutional rights and duties that only need to be asserted to be respected. [Applause.] We surrender without a struggle rights that some of our

[18] "The Future of the Presidency," *The New Republic,* September 29, 1917.

British ancestors died for. I have also reached the conclusion that unreasoning partisanship has something to
do with this growth of a menace to the rights and liberties of the people through breaking down their representatives. . . . When devotion to mere party organization
becomes so strong that principles are forgotten and loyalty
to the instrument of their application is regarded as a
thing of supreme importance, we have reached the danger
line. That view has grown alarmingly in this body. I
have heard members jestingly say that they had raped the
Constitution so often that one more outrage, if in the
party interest, was of small importance. To jest about
the Constitution and the solemn oath we all take to support and defend it is as offensive to the moral sense as
making jokes about a disregard of truth and personal
honesty. But these things help one to understand the con-
tempt with which legislative bodies are treated in the
press and by the public they serve. Yet, in spite of this
yielding attitude, I hope and I believe that the American Congress, which is a great body, representing a
mighty people, will assert itself and will regain its ancient standing and prestige."[19]

[19] Congressional Record, 65th Congress, 3d Session, Vol. 57,
page 1529.

II

EXECUTIVE INITIATIVE IN LEGISLATION; ABROAD

If it is now necessary to reconsider the theory of the separation of governmental powers, and to inquire whether and to what extent the executive officers of the states and the United States should be legally accorded a direct participation in the process of making the laws, by means of the right to initiate and introduce bills in the legislative assemblies, it will be useful to bring to the question a knowledge of the constitutional provisions and parliamentary practices, in this regard, which prevail in the other self-governing countries of the world.

In Great Britain, the government is vested in the Prime Minister and his associates in the cabinet. They maintain themselves in power by the continuous confidence and support of the House of Commons, as manifested by their unbroken control of a substantial majority in that house. Until about the middle of the nineteenth century, the functions of the ministers were chiefly executive, and their rights in regard to the formulation and support of legislative measures were not widely different from those of any other member of Parliament. But following the Reform Act of 1832, the necessity of dealing with the conditions of the times by means of laws of great and wide-spread importance, coupled with the increasing complexity of the details of legislation, almost insensibly led the legislators of England to look to the heads of the great departments of government (having seats in Parliament) as the natural source and origin of new laws, while the centering of both power and responsibility in the cabinet ministers seemed to set them apart as the proper group to assume the framing and engineering of measures of national or imperial importance. Thus the parliamentary system grew. And at present the ministers not only have a recognized precedence in the introduction of bills, but they have a virtual monopoly of the initiative as respects all bills of general public interest.

"Parliament is still, as it was originally intended to be, the grand assize or session of the nation, to criticize and control the government. It is not a council to administer it. It does not originate its own bills, except in minor matters which seem to spring out of public opinion or out of the special circumstances of particular interests, rather than out of the conduct of government. Every legislative proposition of capital importance comes to it from the ministers. The duties of the ministers are not merely executive; the ministers are the government. They look to Parliament, not for commands what to do, but for support in their own programs, whether of legal change or of political policy."[1]

Nothing in the British constitution takes from the private member of Parliament his right to introduce a bill on any subject he may please. And to a limited extent his right is still in exercise. Projects of legislation originating with members who are not in the

[1] Woodrow Wilson, "Constitutional Government in the United States" (1908), p. 84.

ministry are called either "private bills" or "private members' bills." The former are proposed acts dealing with local or individual concerns, very much like the private bills before our state legislatures. The latter are measures having to do with matters of general public concern. Ten or a dozen of such bills may be enacted into law in the course of a legislative year. But for the most part they are non-contentious. It is said that only one or two will arouse such strong differences of opinion as to provoke a demand for a division. A private member with a bill of such a character as not to win general acquiescence has to tread a path beset with difficulties. In the first place, standing orders allot to the disposal of private members so small a part of the time the House is in session—not more than one-tenth of the time of the actual sittings—that there is necessarily keen competition for recognition and opportunity to explain and defend their bills. Again, the course of parliamentary procedure is such that the persistent and determined opposition of even a single member, especially if he be a skillful tactician, will almost invariably block the passage of such a bill. It results, therefore, that the British statutes which have not been fathered by the ministry, but owe their origin to a private member, are few in number and seldom important in character; and that is becoming more and more noticeably the rule.

The present situation has been admirably stated by President Lowell in his authoritative work on "The Government of England,"[2] as follows:

2 Vol. I, p. 326.

"To say that at present the cabinet legislates with the advice and consent of Parliament would hardly be an exaggeration; and it is only the right of private members to bring in a few motions and bills of their own, and to criticize government measures, or propose amendments to them, freely, that prevents legislation from being the work of a mere automatic majority. It does not follow that the action of the cabinet is arbitrary, that it springs from personal judgment divorced from all dependence on popular or parliamentary opinion. The cabinet has its finger always on the pulse of the House of Commons, and especially of its own majority there; and it is ever on the watch for expressions of public feeling outside. Its function is in large part to sum up and formulate the desires of its supporters, but the majority must accept its conclusions, and, in carrying them out, becomes well-nigh automatic."

In view of tendencies in American government already pointed out—the increasing control of the executive over the legislative branch, the increasing disposition to ascribe a sort of special eminence to "administration bills,"—we may find ground for very thoughtful consideration in the last sentence of the extract just quoted. The result of the parliamentary system is that the members of the majority party in the legislature inevitably become mere automata. They must unhesitatingly accept and vote for every measure put forward by the administration. Otherwise they put the ministry in peril and may precipitate its downfall. If they would continue their party and themselves in power, they must let the ministers do their legislative thinking. Even in the matter of amending the cabinet's bills no one has a free hand. To quote again from President Lowell:

"Following upon the responsibility for the introduction and passage of all important measures has come an increasing control by the ministers over the details of their measures. It was formerly maintained that the House could exercise a great deal of freedom in amending bills, without implying a loss of general confidence in the cabinet. But of late, amendments carried against the opposition of the Treasury Bench have been extremely rare. In fact only four such cases have occurred in the last ten years. This does not mean that the debates on the details of bills are fruitless. On the contrary, it often happens that the discussion exposes defects of which the government was not aware, or reveals an unsuspected but wide-spread hostility to some provision; and when this happens the minister in charge of the bill often declares that he will accept an amendment, or undertakes to prepare a clause to meet the objection which has been pointed out. But it does mean that the changes in their bills are made by the ministers themselves after hearing the debate, and that an amendment, even of small consequence, can seldom be carried without their consent. This is the natural outcome of the principle that the cabinet is completely responsible for the principal public measures, and hence must be able to control all their provisions so long as it remains in office."[3]

It must not be forgotten that the tenure of an English ministry is precarious, not fixed, since it depends on the continued support of the House of Commons. The defeat of any important government measure by a decisive majority is accepted as voicing a want of confidence in the ministry. This necessitates the resignation of the cabinet and the formation of a new ministry, and perhaps even the dissolution of Parliament and an appeal to the electorate, with the result that the party returned to power and charged to compose a ministry is regarded as having received a "mandate" from the people as to the particular measure or measures which have been the subject of contention. The

[3] Lowell, "Government of England," Vol. I, p. 317.

English system, then, confides a practical monopoly of
legislation to a small group of men who are at the same
time executive and legislative officers. But along with
this power it imposes on them a complete responsibility. And the measure and mark of their responsibility is their prompt retirement from office if they fail
correctly to interpret the will of the people as represented by a majority in the House of Commons. Can
a similar control of legislation be prudently or even
workably intrusted to any similar group without an
equal responsibility? In other words, would this system be fruitful of good works, supposing the group of
officers placed in control of the making of the laws to
hold office for a fixed term of years, irrespective of
hostile majorities, and to be irremovable save by the
almost impossible process of impeachment?

Similar questions might be asked concerning the
adaptability to American institutions of the parliamentary system of France. The flexibility exhibited in
the making and unmaking of ministries in that country, as contrasted with the fixed tenure of American
executives, is a point sometimes overlooked by those
who desire to invest our President and our governors
with the framing and guidance of legislation. Thus,
it has been said:

"So far as concerns the division of power between the
legislature and the co-ordinate departments, the best organized government in the world today is that of the
French Republic. It is the European government which
has best withstood the shock of war. It successfully
performs that most difficult task of legislation, the tech-
nical task of so framing the law that it shall be enforceable, that it shall actually give effect to the purpose of the

law-maker. It is a significant fact that the legislation of a country where there are few specific constitutional limitations upon legislative power, where there is little reliance upon popular voting and judicial decision to check the flow of undesirable laws, compares in this respect so favorably with that of the American states. The explanation is not far to seek. It lies in the practical monopoly of the initiative in legislation which has been acquired by the executive branch of the government. In France, all important measures are first determined upon by the executive. They are then drafted and the grounds for their adoption elaborated by administrative officials. They are finally introduced into the legislature on behalf of the executive, and their further progress supervised by its agents."[4]

When the executive of France is spoken of, in connection with legislation, it is not the President who is intended, but the ministers. In fact, his position with reference to the ministers of state is exactly opposite to that of an American president in relation to the members of his cabinet. The present President of the French Republic, in an interesting and instructive volume on the government of his country, has said:

"Following the example of England, in 1875, the Republic decided that its President should be responsible only in the event of high treason, and that, on the other hand, the ministers, appointed by him to direct the great public services, should be responsible to the Chambers as a solidarity in matters of general policy and individually for their personal actions. This division of responsibilities is the great characteristic of the constitutional system which is today that of France, and which is known as the parliamentary system. . . . The ministers, in fact, being alone responsible, are those who actually exercise authority; the President presides, but does not govern; he can form no decision save in agreement with his min-

[4] Professor Arthur N. Holcombe, in *The New Republic,* July 7, 1917, p. 270.

isters, and the responsibility is theirs. . . . The President therefore exercises no power alone. Each of his proclamations must be countersigned by a minister."[5]

The third article of the Constitution of 1875 declares that "the President of the Republic shall have the initiative of laws concurrently with the members of the two chambers." But in practice this has come to mean not a direct and personal initiative on the part of the President, but an initiative exercised by him in conjunction with one or more of the ministers, or perhaps, rather, nothing more than his formal assent to an initiative exercised by a minister. For any projected law put forward in the name of the President must be countersigned by a minister, and this minister must thereafter appear in person before the Chambers to explain and defend the measure. The President has no personal access to Parliament and cannot take part in the debates. It might easily result that the President of the French Republic should be only a figurehead, a mere puppet in the hands of his ministers. Historically it is the fact that this does result when he is a man of mediocre gifts. It was Casimir-Perier retiring from office who said that he had been "nothing but a master of ceremonies," and Grevy who described the presidency as merely "an honorable retreat for an old servant of the country." But it is far otherwise with M. Raymond Poincaré, who, bringing to the service of his country in her hour of greatest need, a burning patriotism, ripe wisdom, and brilliant powers of mind, has not failed to impress the stamp of his strong personality upon her contemporary government.

[5] Raymond Poincaré, "How France is Governed" (1914), p. 172.

As in England, there is nothing in the French constitution to deprive senators and deputies who are not members of the ministry of the right to introduce bills; indeed, it is explicitly provided that they shall have the initiative. But, as remarked above, the government has acquired a practical monopoly. A different parliamentary course is followed with a bill presented by a minister from that which prevails in the case of a private member's bill. An administration bill, countersigned by one or more ministers, is at once referred to a commission, composed of a variable number of members, who are instructed to examine it. But a private member's bill is, in the first instance, simply intrusted by him to the "bureau" of the assembly, and is then submitted to a commission known as the Commission of Initiative, which decides whether or not it shall be considered. If it is to be considered, it is referred to a second commission, which thoroughly examines it. The commissions may amend either a bill presented by a minister or one offered by a senator or deputy. In either case they state the result of their labors in a report, and the texts thus prepared are then debated by the Assembly.[6]

By the constitution of the Swiss Confederation the legislative power is vested in the Federal Assembly, which is composed of the National Council and the Council of States. It is provided that "measures may originate in either council and may be introduced by any of their members." "The supreme directive and executive authority of the Confederation shall be exercised by a Federal Council, composed of seven mem-

[6] Raymond Poincaré, "How France is Governed" (1914), p. 218.

bers," and which is presided over by the President of
the Confederation. Also it is declared that the Federal Council "shall introduce bills or resolutions into
the Federal Assembly, and shall give its opinion upon
the proposals submitted to it by the councils or by the
cantons."[7] It will be seen, therefore, that the executive branch of the government is possessed of something more than a mere advisory authority, having a
direct right of initiative; and it is customary practice
for the legislature to invite the executive to prepare
and submit drafts of bills upon important subjects of
legislation.

In those countries of Europe whose form of government is that of a constitutional monarchy, the parliamentary system prevails, with occasional variations
from its English prototype. Indeed there is ground
for arguing that England's greatest gift to the nations of the Continent has been this very system, since
it has enabled free peoples to achieve the highest measure of self-government without revolution and without
discarding the forms of hereditary monarchy. In the
constitutions of those countries, therefore, when we
find the right of initiative in legislation accorded to the
King, it is to be understood that no personal and voli-
tional initiative of the sovereign is intended, but an
initiative exercised by responsible ministers in the
name of the titular ruler, just as, in England, the laws
are still supposed to be made by the King with the
advice and consent of the Lords and Commons.

In the Netherlands, it is constitutionally provided
that "the King shall recommend projects of law to the

[7] Swiss Constitution of 1874, arts. 93, 95, 102.

States-General, and make such other recommendations to them as he considers proper. He shall have the right to approve or to reject the laws adopted by the States-General," and "the States-General shall have the power to present projects of law to the King. But the initiative in this regard shall belong exclusively to the lower house."[8] In Belgium, "the legislative power shall be exercised collectively by the King, the House of Representatives, and the Senate. Each of the three branches of the legislative power shall have the right of initiative. Nevertheless all laws relating to the revenues or expenditures of the state or to the army contingent must be voted first by the House of Representatives."[9] In Denmark, "the King may submit to the Rigsdag projects of laws and of other measures."[10] In Sweden, "if the King wishes to propose a bill to the Riksdag, he shall obtain the opinion of the Council of State and of the Supreme Court regarding the matter, and shall present his proposal, together with such opinions, to the Riksdag."[11] In Norway, "every bill shall be first presented in the Odelsthing [lower house] either by one of its members or by the government through a councillor of state."[12] By the constitution of Italy, "the initiative in legislation shall belong both to the King and the two houses. But all bills imposing taxes or relating to the budget shall first be presented to the House of Deputies."[13] In Spain, "the King

[8] Netherlands, Constitution of 1887, arts. 71, 116, 117.
[9] Belgium, Constitution of 1831, arts. 26, 27.
[10] Denmark, Constitution of 1866, art. 23.
[11] Sweden, Constitution of 1809, art. 87.
[12] Norway, Constitution of 1814, art. 76.
[13] Italy, Constitution of 1848, art. 10.

and each of the legislative bodies shall have the right
to initiate laws. Laws relating to taxation and to the
public credit shall be presented in the first instance in
the Congress of Deputies."[14] And the constitution of
Japan contains a provision that "both houses shall
vote upon projects of law submitted to them by the
government, and may respectively initiate projects of
law."[15]

The countries of Latin America offer a most interesting field for the study in which we are engaged, because they have generally tried, in their constitutions,
to combine the essential features of the North American or "presidential system" of government with some
important details of the European or "parliamentary"
system. That is, while they have set up a chief executive vested with powers and duties corresponding
with those of the President of the United States, and
holding office for a fixed term and practically irremovable, they have also bestowed upon him (acting either
personally or through his ministers) a direct access to
the legislative bodies and the right of initiative therein,
with the necessary result that his control over legislation is always a factor of serious importance, and may
at any time become formidable. Both South American and European writers have seen in this attempt
to blend two incompatible systems the chief cause of
the conspiracies and revolutions which have too often
disgraced the history of those countries. For, in their
view, it leads to such a hypertrophy of the executive
power—especially when the prestige of the president

[14] Spain, Constitution of 1876, art. 41.
[15] Japan, Constitution of 1889, art. 38.

and his most powerful ministers is based upon military exploits or maintained by the army—as cannot fail to be a constant menace to the state. That it may make possible a self-perpetuating and absolutistic dictatorship (benevolent or otherwise) is abundantly shown by the history of Porfirio Diaz in Mexico.

The following may suffice as a brief summary of the constitutional provisions on this point to be found in Central and South America: In the Argentine, Haiti, and Paraguay, the right of initiative is given to the members of the two houses of the legislature and also to "the executive" or "the executive power." In Chile, "laws may be initiated in the Senate or in the House of Deputies upon the motion of any member or by message of the President of the Republic," and the same provision is found in Bolivia, with the additional requirement that a bill submitted by the President "shall be supported in the debates by at least one of the cabinet ministers, but he shall have no vote." In Costa Rica and Uruguay, in addition to the initiative of the members of the legislature, laws may originate "on the proposal of the executive power through the medium of the secretaries of state." In Colombia and Panama, the initiative is not given directly to the President, but it is given to the cabinet ministers or secretaries of state. In Ecuador, "the laws, decrees, and resolutions of Congress may originate in either of the chambers on the proposal of any of its members, or of the executive power, or of the Supreme Court in so far as concerns the administration of justice," and substantially the same provision is found in the constitutions of Guatemala, Peru, the Dominican Republic, Salvador, Nicaragua, and Honduras, except that in the three last-named countries a bill may be introduced not directly by the President but through a minister or secretary of state. In Mexico, "the right to originate legislation pertains to the President of the Republic, to the representatives and senators of the Congress, and to the state legislatures. Bills submitted by the President of the Republic, by state legislatures, or by delegations of the states, shall be at once referred to committees. Those introduced by representatives or senators shall be subject to the rules of procedure." Brazil and Cuba have more directly followed the example of the United States, and do not permit the direct initiation of legislation by the executive or the ministers.

III

EXECUTIVE INITIATIVE IN LEGISLATION; IN THE UNITED STATES

Should the American people now cast overboard the political principle so jealously insisted on by their ancestors, that it is essential to the preservation of civil liberty that the executive and legislative powers of the state should be kept separate and distinct? Should we now attempt the experiment of superimposing upon the present structure of our government the chief features of the parliamentary or cabinet system as practiced in England and France, as least to the extent of formally giving to the executive officers of the nation and the states direct access to the legislative bodies, the right to frame and introduce their own bills, to claim precedence for administration measures, to support them in debate, and to expedite and secure their passage with the weight and power of the executive arm?

It is very seriously proposed, and by persons whose opinions are entitled to the highest respect, that just this should be done. Even so wise and conservative a statesman as ex-Governor McCall of Massachusetts, if correctly quoted in an interview published not long since,[1] thinks that

"we cannot amble along in this country on the very pleasant pathway of the old theory of division of powers,

[1] The New York *Times*, Magazine Section, July 22, 1917.

so that one organ of government vetoes another and we have difficulty in getting anywhere. In a crisis like the present, when the safety of the country depends on the promptest possible action in preparation for war, a ministry responsible to an elected assembly would bring forward the measures that in its judgment are required; and while these measures would be open to debate and amendment, they would be pressed to a speedy conclusion and there would not be the dawdling that has been witnessed at Washington. Debate is a good thing, and ample opportunity should be given for it; but the expansion and dilution of individual views do not inevitably throw light on questions. The administration measures in times like these should not only have a right of way, but a really efficient system of government would provide that a decision might be obtained in something like a reasonable time."

Disclaiming any intention to advocate the substitution of the British cabinet system of government for our present form, Mr. McCall added:

"I think we should have something in the development of our system that would give to an administration the right to present its policies in an authoritative manner, so far as the administration is concerned, and the interests of the people would require that these policies should be either approved or disapproved by Congress seasonably, so that they would not become obsolete or of very much less importance on account of the long delay. I think there has been too much individualism at Washington. The right of individual members of a legislative body should, of course, yield to the general right and needs."

The questions propounded above, as to changes in our legislative methods, are not merely of academic interest; they are of immediate practical importance. And as a matter of fact, in the national government, a disposition which grew into a tendency, and a tendency which grew into a habit, have already brought about the establishment of something very like the parliamentary system of executive initiative and control of bills, not so much in substitution for the methods contemplated by the Constitution as in addition to them. Today it is not at all an uncommon practice for a legislative measure, complete in all its details, to be drafted by the head of an executive department, or even by the President or under his personal direction, and submitted to Congress through the chairman of the appropriate committee or some other member known to be a supporter of the administration, and to be followed up by such executive pressure as will secure its proper reference and its ultimate enactment into law. It has been said:

"In the United States the failure openly to give to the President constitutional powers by the exercise of which he can influence the passage of legislation and the adoption of policies, has naturally led to the development of somewhat secret and indirect, if not underhand, methods. The President cannot introduce a bill into Congress. But there is nothing to prevent him from having a bill drawn and inducing one of his supporters in Congress to introduce it. The President has no power to send a representative of the administration to participate in the debates of Congress. But members of the administration are often heard by the committees of Congress to which bills are referred, and the President may easily persuade some member of the legislature to be his spokesman on the floor of either of the houses."[2]

These facts are familiar to everyone who reads the newspapers, though it may be doubted whether many of us realize the extent to which the habit has grown. That it may be seen in practice, though not in its full

[2] Frank J. Goodnow, "Principles of Constitutional Government," p. 121.

extent, attention is invited to the following extracts
from the daily press, which, however, do not pretend
to be a list or catalogue, but only a few illustrations
culled out of many:

"At the request of the War Department today Chairman Chamberlain of the Senate military committee introduced a bill for the registration for military duty of all
ment who have become twenty-one years old since the
draft law went into effect.   Another bill which Senator
Chamberlain introduced at the request of the administration would provide for furloughing National Army
men for harvesting crops and other agricultural duty."

Again: "An administration bill authorizing the President to suspend, modify, or annul sentences and orders
of military courts-martial was submitted yesterday by
Secretary Baker to Chairman Chamberlain of the Senate
military committee."   On another occasion, "Representative Adamson introduced with amendments the President's bill to authorize preferential food shipments by
rail and water."   So again: "The Overman bill, prepared by the President or at his direction, and sent from
the White House to the Capitol, is a proposal to Congress
to abdicate during the period of the war and for one year
after the war."   And again: "Personal interest of President Wilson in the clause in the espionage bill authorizing him to embargo exports was disclosed today during
debate on the bill in the Senate.   A letter from the President to Chairman Culberson of the Senate judiciary committee, submitting a draft of the bill and urging its consideration, was produced and read."

And a prominent member of the House of Representatives is reported to have said in debate recently:

"The fashion has been growing of late, particularly
when bills of major importance are being considered in
this House, that their sponsors rest their main ground
of defense of the provisions of these bills upon the proposition that they were drafted in some executive department.   Things have come to a pretty pass in this country

if legislation is to be simply a matter of executive order, if committees of this House are to be a mere registering machine for the will of the executive. For one, I believe that the time has come to definitely impress upon the executive and upon the country that we propose to do some thinking for ourselves, that we propose to scrutinize rigidly the legislative proposals sent to us from the other end of the Avenue, and to enact them with such additions, subtractions or alterations as seem best to us, acting in the capacity imposed upon us by the Constitution; in short, that we propose to conduct ourselves as the legislative representatives of the American people, and not simply as the amanuenses of those holding executive office."

So much for the initiation of administration bills. But the executive does not abandon a favorite project at the threshold of the legislative chamber. On the contrary, he is quite actively interested in its further fortunes and brings to bear many processes of influence and persuasion to insure its enactment. In the first place, the administration's proposal that a particular law should be passed may and often does take a much stronger form than the mere "recommendation" intended by the Constitution. The members of Congress may be assured, by message or letter, as sometimes they have been, that the measure in question is "absolutely necessary" to the accomplishment of some purpose as to whose desirability there can be no possible dispute. Or, in the converse case, private initiative may be checked by a frank expression of stern disapproval from the presidential mansion. Again, whatever may have been the antique practice of a mutual and dignified aloofness, the modern American President is in constant and free communication with the chairmen of important committees in both houses,

with the parliamentary leaders of the party, with his
individual friends and supporters, and even with those
who are most conspicuous in their opposition to his
policies. It has become a common practice, no longer
exciting surprise or even comment, for the President
to summon influential members of either house to a
conference at the White House, nor is it a secret that
the purpose is to settle the details of an administration bill or to concert ways and means for securing its
passage, or perhaps to block the pathway of independent insurgents. Nor have the occasions been infre-
quent in which the President has himself gone to the
room set apart for him at the Capitol and there summoned to his presence Senators or Representatives
whose strong opposition threatened disaster to some
favored measure. The object of such interviews is
of course the taking of common counsel for the welfare of the country. But is it not the case that when
the legislators return to their seats, their votes reflect
the wishes of the executive?

Again, always supposing that presidential insistence
upon the enactment of particular bills or provisions is
recognized as constitutionally within the functions of
the executive, what could be more natural than that he
should employ his most trusted friends and advisers,
the members of the cabinet, as his advocates before
Congress? As a matter of fact, recent Presidents
have not hesitated to do so. It may be appropriate to
quote one or two events of late occurrence, not at all
in the way of hostile criticism, but simply as illustrations of this system in its actual operation. In the
news columns of a leading newspaper we read the following:

"The influence of President Wilson's approval of the newspaper censorship section of the espionage bill failed to save it in the House today, and it was stricken from the bill by a vote of 220 to 167. The vote came after administration leaders had fought for the section under a hot fire of attack, and Chairman Webb of the judiciary committee had told the House he had just heard from President Wilson that the section was necessary to the defense and safety of the country. Postmaster General Burleson, who often visits the Capitol to round up support for administration measures, made a futile attempt to get enough support for the censorship section. . . . Representative Webb did everything in his power to rally to his support enough votes to give the administration almost unheard-of power in proclaiming what may or may not be published. Postmaster General Burleson was in the corridors and lobbies of the House for several hours today in a vain attempt to preserve the censorship section by telling members on both sides of the House that the administration absolutely demanded it."[8]

In a parallel case of somewhat later date, an Associated Press despatch carried the following account of certain proceedings in the Senate:

"Opponents of the Overman bill, to authorize the President to reorganize government departments and agencies for the war period, opened their attack today in the Senate. . . . While Senator Reed was speaking, Postmaster General Burleson, who took the Overman bill to the Capitol the day it was introduced, appeared in the President's room just outside the Senate chamber, and conferred with a number of supporters of the measure. Referring to Mr. Burleson's visit, the Missouri Senator declared he would not object to replying to cabinet members' arguments if they were made on the floor of the Senate rather than in whispered conversations in the cloak rooms."

Finally, anyone who seeks the causes of the Presi-

[8] The Washington *Evening Star*, May 4, 1917.

dent's ascendancy over Congress should not overlook his negative upon laws which he disapproves.

"The veto power," it has been well said, "taken in connection with the message and the appointing power, is an effective political instrument in the hands of the President. By using a threat of the veto he may secure the passage of bills which he personally favors, and at all times, in considering important measures, Congress must keep in view the possible action of the President, especially where it is a party question and the correct attitude before the country is indispensable. Mr. Roosevelt even went so far as to warn Congress publicly that he would not sign certain measures then before that body, and raised a storm of protest from those who said that he should not veto a bill until it was laid before him."[4]

In fine, the recital of the foregoing considerations will have been futile indeed if the reader is not now prepared to agree with the statement that a legalized practice of admitting executive officers directly to the legislative body would "make unnecessary those *subterranean* relations between the two branches which inevitably spring up when official lines of communication are forbidden."[5]

For the real and ultimate question is, shall these subterranean, underhand, and extra-constitutional methods be legalized or shall they be abandoned?

It is difficult to reverse an evolutionary process, and what we have been describing appears to be a true political evolution. If so, even the incumbency of a President who should keep himself strictly within the bounds of the Constitution (in its spirit and meaning no less than its letter) would be no more than an inter-

[4] Charles A. Beard, "American Government and Politics," p. 204.

[5] "Municipal Research," May, 1915, p. 75.

ruption of a practice which his successor would very likely resume and carry to even greater lengths. For there is nothing in the text of the Constitution which forbids the President to dominate Congress. There is nothing to forbid him to write out with his own hand the complete draft of a bill and send it to a friend to be introduced in the Senate or the House. There is nothing to prevent him from exerting every penny-weight of his prestige, his personal influence, and his political power in favor of its enactment. There is nothing unlawful in his sending his ministers to the field of legislative battle. There is nothing to prevent him from laying out a program for the legislature to follow. There is nothing to restrain him from bend-ing the frown of his disapproval upon individual ini-tiative. In short (be it said without disrespect) there is nothing to withhold him from being the most august and powerful of all lobbyists, and the most successful. Even if constitutional warrant against some or any of these practices could be found, one can hardly see how the matter could be brought to the arbitrament of the courts.

To these tendencies and practices there is nothing to oppose but the remonstrances of individual members of Congress—which are sonorous but ineffectual—or the general disapproval of the people of the country. If such a sentiment were ever to be aroused, it would require such a change of heart in the American public that they would cease to magnify the presidential office, and no longer exalt the President as the nation's leader, but restore the guardianship of the public wel-fare to its original custodians, the members of the

Congress, taking care to select such representatives as would ably and conscientiously fullfil their trust. But the American people, with the watchword "efficiency" forever ringing in the air, demand only results from their government. To methods and processes they are sublimely indifferent.

It may be thought that this view is unduly pessimistic. It is not meant to be denied that there are alert sentinels, here and there, to cry the alarm. And some of them believe that, not their voices alone, but the daily spectacle of executive power in action, has so far impinged upon the consciousness of their fellow citizens as to awaken at least a feeling of deep concern. Thus, Professor Henry Jones Ford writes:

"The most dangerous feature of the situation is the present attitude of public opinion. The behavior of Congress is a chronic grievance, but it does not produce action at all commensurate with the feeling that exists about the matter. This singular lethargy is due to the fact that resentment of congressional behavior is overshadowed by uneasiness over the portentous growth of presidential authority. People view with dismay the possibilities of abuse of such vast powers as are accumulating in the hands of the President. They feel disposed to endure much from Congress in consideration of the fact that it appears to be a rival power, and in the belief that, badly as it behaves in particulars, it serves as a counterpoise to the aggrandizement of the presidential office. The same view is held in Congress, and members who acknowledge that its powers are scandalously abused are yet disposed to put up with anything rather than do anything that might weaken those powers. This view of the case is plausible, but it is quite mistaken. It is true that the power of the President has increased and is increasing at a tremendous rate; but the constitutional aspect of the case is quite different from what is commonly supposed. The great expansion of the presidential function is going on outside of the formal Constitution, by reason of his enforced activity as lobbyist and promoter. His authority within the bounds of the Constitution has not increased at all, but has in fact been diminished by congressional encroachment, and that is the true source of actual peril to constitutional government."[6]

Precisely because all this is going on outside the formal Constitution, it would require no change in the fundamental law either to abandon it or to legalize it. No constitutional amendment would be necessary to render legal and formally regular an even greater presidential control over legislation than is now practised in a somewhat furtive and unacknowledged manner. It is correctly said by Professor Ford, at the conclusion of the article from which the foregoing quotation is taken:

"This is a matter which rests with Congress, and it is upon Congress that the pressure of public opinion should be exerted to compel such changes in the rules as will introduce constitutional government. In practice this would mean that the President's recommendations would be presented to Congress in the form of bills drafted by experts, informed by administrative experience and acting under national responsibility. The present method allows legislation to be drafted according to the views of irresponsible committees acting under the guidance of particular interests and upon calculations of factional advantage. The sinister results of which this process is capable are displayed by the legislative record of every session. The situation has become so intolerable that some decisive treatment of it is inevitable."

In another paper, the same author has expressed himself still more explicitly, as follows:

"The fact is well known that the policy of the administration is the master force that advances measures and

[6] "The Growth of Dictatorship," in *The Atlantic Monthly*, May, 1918.

brings them to determination. Well, then, let it be so;
but is there not room for improvement? At present the
process goes on in the dark. Conflicting and vague accounts reach the public of conferences with party leaders,
of negotiations with committees, of caucus action, of concessions and adjustments to placate dissident factions, of
delays, obstructions, exactions and demands which must
be dealt with to obtain action. It is a dark, confused
hubbub of activity, the particular elements of which can
never be clearly discerned by the public, nor can the extent of their respective participation in what is done be
computed. Moreover it appears that Congress itself is
not much better situated for knowing just what is taking
place. Enactments may contain features of which Congress was not aware in passing them, their presence being due to private opportunity supplied by the darkness in
which bills take their final shape. Notorious instances
of this occurred during the last session of Congress. Is
not this darkness a genuine grievance that calls for re-
dress? What improvement could be more natural and
desirable than to bring the process out of darkness into
light? The specific demand for improvement in legislative procedure need therefore go no further than this:
that the administration shall propose and explain all its
measures—the bills and the budget—openly in Congress
and fix the time when they shall be considered and put
to vote. That is all, no more and no less. Aside from
those particulars, the existing deposit of authority, both
with the President and with Congress, will remain unimpaired. There will be no change whatever except this
one change caused by making the administration do openly and publicly what it now does hiddenly and privately.
Undoubtedly this one change will breed more change, but
that will come spontaneously under the prompting of
party convenience. Just what form the adjustments
will eventually assume cannot be anticipated, and specu-
lation on this point is sheer futility. All that it is safe to
say is that it will not be the parliamentary type of government as in England. The definite term and the independent authority of the presidential office is a solid
circumstance that will condition all our constitutional de-

velopment. The eventual type will probably differ from any existing type of government. It will be a distinctly American type, the product of our own needs and experiences."[7]

A similar opinion has recently been expressed by Professor Freund.

"It is not uncommonly urged at the present time that executive officers be given a right to appear on the floor of the houses of the legislature and to participate in debate. It would not be a much more radical step to give the chief executive a right to introduce bills. He has now by all constitutions the right to recommend legislation, and as a matter of power there is no reason why he should not present his recommendations in the form of bills. This would not give the measure recommended the parliamentary status of a bill, and as a matter of politics, might prejudice it; but to give it such a status would not even require a constitutional amendment; a house rule would be sufficient. As a matter of fact, the chief executive can readily find members to bring in bills known to have come from him and spoken of as administration bills, and they have been officially recognized as such by house rules, but their status would gain if the executive would formally appear as their sponsor."[8]

President Wilson, also, some ten years ago, observed that there is no reason to believe that the framers of the Constitution

"meant actually to exclude the President from all intimate personal consultation with the houses in session. No doubt the President and the members of his cabinet could with perfect legal propriety, and without any breach of the spirit of the Constitution, attend the sessions of either the House or the Senate and take part in their discussions, at any rate to the extent of answering questions and explaining any measures which the Presi-

[7] Henry Jones Ford, "A Program of Responsible Democracy," in American Political Science Review, August, 1918, p. 494.

[8] "Standards of American Legislation," p. 291.

dent might see fit to urge in the message which the Constitution explicitly authorizes him to send to Congress."[9]

And another student of American government, in discussing the subject has said:

"Instances are not wanting of the transmission to Congress, by the executive, of drafts of bills, with a recommendation for their enactment. As Professor Burgess states, there is full constitutional warrant for the construction and presentation of regular bills and projects of laws to Congress by the President. That his recommendations are not so presented has explanation in the fact that there exist no 'executive organs for presenting, explaining, defending, and in general managing such government bills in Congress.' This custom of initiating and promoting legislation in this manner might have grown up under our Constitution. Says Professor Woodburn: 'If Hamilton, in defending his financial measures before Congress in 1790, had appeared in person instead of sending a written report, it is conceivable that the precedent might have been followed, and the cabinet ministers might have been allowed the privilege of defending their measures on the floor of either house.' "[10]

Arguments are not wanting in favor of conceding to the executive branch of the government the formal right to initiate and introduce bills, particularly if we take into account the inevitable result of such a concession, namely, that the executive will sooner or later come to have a virtual monopoly of the initiative. In the first place, it would render possible the carrying out of a definite program of legislation for each Congress or each session of Congress. Under the present system, an enormous number of bills are annually cast into the hopper, the committees are overburdened, the calendars are crowded, there is jostling and scrambling

[9] "Constitutional Government in the United States," p. 201.
[10] Finley, "The American Executive," p. 201.

for precedence, unworthy methods of recruiting support for favorite measures are brought into play, and
the device of special rules is resorted to for the purpose of cutting down opposition or choking criticism.
Only the great appropriation bills are sure to pass, and
these are sometimes encumbered with absurdly irrelevant "riders." The task of sifting the mass of legislative projects and sorting out a limited number, with
the determination that they must be enacted before the
close of the session, is at present very imperfectly performed by "steering committees" in the two houses,
and not without a view to the political prosperity of
the dominant party. Another advantage could be
found in the elimination of a system which permits,
and indeed encourages, the wasteful duplication of
bills on the same subject. When public attention is
focussed upon some state of affairs which seems to
require regulation by act of Congress, it is no uncommon thing for half a dozen or more bills to be offered
in the House and perhaps two or three in the Senate,
all differing in details and to a certain extent in their
general principles. These are all referred to the appropriate committees; each committee attempts to har-
monize or consolidate the measures before it, and,
generally failing in this, the committee drafts and presents a new bill; these are passed in the two houses,
but are so dissimilar as to require a conference; and
not infrequently the conference committee draws up
what is substantially a new bill, and this is finally enacted. All this could be avoided if an administration
bill, exempt from competition with privately initiated
measures on the same subject, were introduced, simul-

taneously and in identical language, in the two houses. Such a system would also reduce the number of projects to be placed before the legislature, increase the relative importance of those scheduled for consideration, concentrate and solidify the opposition, and avoid the occurrence of those legislative freaks (not unknown in Congress, though more common in the states) which arouse the disrespectful and injurious derision of the public.

And there is no doubt whatever that the technique of bill-drafting would be greatly improved. That there is ample room for improvement could be shown with ease from almost any volume of the Statutes at Large. But one or two illustrations will suffice. Let it be remembered, for instance, that the Bankruptcy Act of 1898 contains two clauses relating to the same subject which the courts have pronounced absolutely repugnant and irreconcilable. One clause was contained in the bill as originally passed by the House, and the other in the bill as originally passed by the Senate, and both were retained by the conference committee which settled the terms of the statute in its final form, and consequently passed by both houses without adverting to the conflict between them. Again, it will not have been forgotten that the Income Tax Act of 1913 was one of the crudest pieces of legislation known in our history, being singularly infelicitous in its language, confused in its arrangement, and in places entirely unintelligible.

This subject has been remarkably well elucidated by Professor Freund, in a recent notable volume, from which we quote as follows:

"The striking difference between legislation abroad and in this country is that under every system except the American the executive government has a practical monopoly of the legislative initiative. In consequence, the preparation of bills becomes the business of government officials responsible to ministers, these government officials being mainly, if not exclusively, employed in constructive legislative work. In France and Germany, the government initiative of legislation has been established for a long time, and the right of members to introduce bills is hedged about and practically negligible. There are two main reasons why executive initiative should lead to a superior legislative product. The one is that it is the inevitable effect of professionalizing a function that its standards are raised. The draftsman will take a pride in his business and in course of time will become an expert in it. He learns from experience, and traditions will be formed. This, of course, presupposes that he is a permanent official. In addition, he will be responsible to his chief, who naturally resents drafting defects that expose him to parliamentary non-partisan criticism. In Germany, the best juristic talent that goes into the government service is utilized for the preparation of legislative products, and these are regularly accompanied by exhaustive statements of reasons, which enjoy considerable authority. Drafts of important measures are almost invariably published long before they go to the legislature, in order to receive the widest criticism, and, as the result of criticism, are often revised and sometimes entirely withdrawn. The individual author often remains unknown and the credit of the government stands behind the work. The second reason is that when the government introduces a bill, the parliamentary debate is somewhat in the nature of an adversary procedure, or at least there is, as it were, a petitioner and a judge. The minister or his representative (in Germany and France, the experts appear in parliament as commissioners, while in England only parliamentary secretaries may speak— much to the disadvantage of the English debate) has to defend the measure against criticism, and legal imperfections or inequities would be legitimate grounds of attack.

The liability to criticism insures proper care in advance. Together with the executive initiative goes a practical limitation of the number of bills introduced, an increased relative importance of each measure and proportionately greater attention bestowed on it. Where this form of legislative preparation and procedure has been observed, it is not necessary to seek further reasons for a good quality of the product."[11]

To this it may be added that hardly any statute is so completely *res nova* that it does not to some extent modify the existing law and therefore require to be carefully co-ordinated with the previous enactments. Almost every new law should be neatly dovetailed into an existing structure of legislation; and many a legislative blunder is due to a neglect of this simple fact.

Of course it may be replied to these arguments and considerations that it is not necessary to give to the executive officers of government a monopoly of legislative initiative, or even a share in it, in order to secure scientific precision and clarity in the preparation of bills. For any legislative body or chamber may, if it chooses, establish a bill-drafting bureau and fill it with the most expert talent available. But it is less easy to dispose of the fact pointed out by Mr. Wilson, that if those who frame the laws are then charged with the duty of seeing to their application in actual practice, they will be more careful in the details of what they enact.

"Under the parliamentary form of government," he says, "the people's recognized leaders for the time being, that is, the leaders of the political party which for the time commands a majority in the popular house of parliament, are both heads of the executive and guides of the

[11] Ernst Freund, "Standards of American Legislation," p. 288.

legislature. They both conduct government and suggest legislation. All the chief measures of a parliamentary session originate with them, and they are under the sobering necessity of putting into successful execution the laws they propose."[12]

On the other hand, it cannot be gainsaid that the inevitable tendency of the cabinet or parliamentary system of government is to vest a monopoly of legislative initiative in the executive. It may not be so intended. It is perhaps never so specified in any constitution or law. On the contrary, wherever the system is in force the right of private initiative remains theoretically unimpaired. But actually it dwindles, while the executive initiative grows, until the former is restricted to local and trifling matters, and the latter controls all measures of real importance. Thus the legislative debates become mere exhibitions of attack and defense, the function of the opposition is limited to criticism, and the administration's bills are carried by a majority which works automatically. If this system appears to work well in Great Britain, and less obviously so in France, it is by no means certain that it is at all adapted to political conditions in the United States, to our institutions, or to the habits of thought and action characteristic of our people. It is, as Lord Bryce has said, not a plant of hardy growth nor certain to flourish in an alien ground.

"This system of so-called cabinet government," he observes, "seems to Europeans now, who observe it at work over a large part of the world, an obvious and simple system. We are apt to forget that it was never seen anywhere till the English developed it by slow degrees, and

[12] Woodrow Wilson, "Constitutional Government in the United States" (1908), p. 40.

that it is a very delicate system, depending on habits, traditions, and understandings which are not easily set forth in words, much less transplanted to a new soil. . . . It is a system whose successful working presupposes the existence of two great parties and no more, parties each strong enough to restrain the violence of the other, yet one of them steadily preponderant in any given House of Commons. Where a third, perhaps a fourth, party appears, the conditions are changed. The scales of Parliament oscillate as the weight of this detached group is thrown on one side or the other; dissolutions become more frequent, and even dissolutions may fail to restore stability. The recent history of the French Republic shows the difficulties of working a chamber composed of groups, nor is the same source of difficulty unknown in England."[13]

Other countries than England and France have tried the parliamentary system, apparently with very dubious success. In Spain, for example, the actual operation of the system is thus described by a publicist of that country:

"The attention of the chambers being demanded for so many affairs foreign to the mission of the legislative power, they have not time to devote themselves to an examination of the laws. The discussion of records, discussion of the message, questions and interpellations every day, all this absorbs a month and a half or two months, which is the average length of time during which the Cortes remain open in each legislature. In the last sittings they approve in mass the railroad bills, and likewise the accounts of the State and the budgets, almost without examining them, and, at best, with only a pretense of discussion. When the administration proposes to inaugurate reforms in legislation, civil, penal, administrative, commercial, etc., they ask the Cortes for an authorization, and with this subterfuge the ministers legislate at their own caprice, just as the absolute kings used to legislate at will. Only laws of a notably politi-

[13] Bryce, "American Commonwealth" (1889), pp. 272, 281.

cal character have the privilege of occupying the attention of the chambers."[14]

In the next place, we must by no means forget that the very essence of the parliamentary system is the responsibility of the ministers, who must resign when confronted with a hostile majority against an administration measure of first-rate rank. Make the executive irremovable, and this responsibility becomes attenuated to the degree where it is no more than an uneasy apprehension as to the state of public opinion, that opinion being diffuse and unorganized and not capable of becoming articulate for perhaps two or three years. We may repeat the doubts expressed on a previous page, as to whether a control of legislation similar to that held by the ministry in England could be prudently or even practically intrusted to any similar group in this country without the same or an equal kind and measure of responsibility, or whether the cabinet system would result in wise, just, and beneficent government, supposing the executive officers placed in control of the output of legislation to hold office for a fixed term of years, irrespective of hostile majorities, and to be removable in no other way than by impeachment.

The confusion of the executive with the legislative power, or the possession of them both by the same individual or group, always leads, as Montesquieu foresaw it would, to dictatorship. The rule of the dictator may be wise or unwise, benevolent or tyrannical,

[14] Ojea y Somoza ("El Parlamentarismo") as quoted by Miñana, "La Division de los Poderes del Estado" (Madrid, 1917), p. 219.

promotive of the public welfare or ruinous to his country; but the event depends upon his character and his will, not upon the constitution of the country. Even in England,

"one may say that the legislative and executive functions are interwoven as closely under this system as under absolute monarchies, such as imperial Rome or modern Russia; and the fact that taxation, while effected by means of legislation, is the indispensable engine of administration, shows how inseparable are these two apparently distinct powers."[15]

In sober truth, as remarked by a Spanish writer,

"in many countries parliamentarism is a screen behind which lurks the absolutism of royalty-by-the-grace-of-God. Where it is a reality, where the parliament reigns and governs in fact, it signifies nothing else than the dictatorship of certain personages, who alternately grasp the reins of power. In effect, these are found to be in the hands of a half dozen party chiefs with their counsellors and acolytes."[16] Again: "There is a manifest tendency to favor arbitrary power, because what results is the substitution, in place of the ancient absolutism of an individual, of the absolutism of a group, or even of a single individual again, the chief of a party. For if, after centralizing the administration and placing it in the hands of the executive power, the legislature converts itself into a sort of workshop for that power, the ministers are lords and masters of the situation, without other hindrance or inconvenience than that of suffering the pin-pricks of the press, and of defending themselves with a few sophisms against the attacks of the opposition in the chambers."[17]

And further, as specially illustrating the situation in Spain, but not without a general application, we may quote the observation that

[15] Bryce, "American Commonwealth" (1889), p. 272.
[16] Miñana, "La Division de los Poderes del Estado," p. 208.
[17] Idem, p. 221.

"absolutism pure and simple, without a parliament, has after all the one good condition that the sovereign always retains a personal sense of responsibility for his own acts. Much worse is the absolutism which can buttress itself upon a docile parliament, and which needs no other justification than that of appealing to the assent of a majority. Houses constituted under such a system of parliamentarism would have been the ideal senate for the Emperor Tiberius."[18]

Finally, it cannot be inappropriate to listen to a counsel of prudence from one who, having filled the office of President of the United States, has left on record his impressions of its duties and opportunities.

"It is true that a parliamentary government offers an opportunity for greater effectiveness, in that the same mind or minds control the executive and the legislative action, and the one can be closely suited to the other; whereas our President has no initiative in respect to legislation given him by law except that of mere recommendation, and no method of entering into the argument and discussion of the proposed legislation while pending in Congress, except that of a formal message or address. To one charged with the responsibilities of the President, especially where he has party pledges to perform, this seems a defect; but whatever I thought while in office, I am inclined now to think that the defect is more theoretical than actual."[19]

It is possibly worthy of suggestion, however, that we might profit by the example of European countries, and even of some of our Latin-American neighbors, to the extent of having administration measures, properly so called, drafted, introduced, and managed on the floor by members of the administration, and those relating to the organization, jurisdiction, and duties of

[18] Sanchez de Toca ("La Crisis de Nuestro Parlamentarismo") as quoted by Miñana, op. cit., p. 234.
[19] William H. Taft, "Our Chief Magistrate," p. 11.

the judiciary by the justices of the Supreme Court. But the term "administration measures," in this sense, would not include all bills favored by the executive or originating in his recommendations, but only those relating to the administration of government, that is, to the organization, powers, duties, and relations of the different departments, bureaus, and commissions. In this way, as also in regard to bills relating to the courts, the highest expert talent would be employed in preparing the measures for the consideration of Congress, and those best qualified by experience would be engaged in explaining and defending them. Under such a plan as this, a bill to create a Department of Munitions, or one to define the powers of the Interstate Commerce Commission, or one to regulate proceedings in the General Land Office, would be drafted and sponsored by those best qualified to undertake the task, while such an act as that which created the Circuit Courts of Appeals would have been prepared under the direct supervision of the Supreme Court, to the obvious advantage, in every instance, of those most interested in promoting the scientific accuracy and precision of such pieces of legislation, and eventually of the country at large.

IV

THE CABINET IN CONGRESS

The proposal that the members of the President's cabinet should be given the right of direct access to the floor of the two houses of Congress is not regarded by those who favor it as at all inimical to the philosophical principle in government of the separation of the executive and legislative powers. On the contrary, it is urged as a step to be taken in the direction of bringing about a closer harmony and better co-ordination in the work of the two departments. Nevertheless, if the relations between the President and the Congress are in a state of unstable equilibrium, and if the balance has of late years been inclining in favor of the power of the President,—and that, with an accelerating motion almost comparable to that of a body falling in air,—and if it has already become an established custom for the President to use the members of the cabinet as his most powerful advocates and intermediaries in procuring from Congress what he desires or blocking what he opposes, as we have tried to show in the foregoing pages, then the proposal in question must be studied as a factor in the constant struggle of the executive branch of government for ascendancy and control. In its narrowest form the project intends merely that the cabinet ministers should have a legal right to go upon the floor of the Senate

or House and participate at will in the debates.   In
its widest form, there is added the proposition that
they should have the right to introduce bills of their
own drafting, that they should be required to attend
the sittings of Congress either on call for their presence or on stated days, and that they should be under
the obligation to furnish information and to answer
questions concerning matters pending in, or which may
affect, their several departments.

Though this subject is of special importance at the
present moment, it is not a new thing in our history.
As far back as 1881, a select committee of the Senate
recommended the passage of an act giving the heads
of departments access to the floor of the houses, with
the right to introduce bills and to support them in debate.   The report of the committee was signed by Senators Pendleton, Allison, Voorhees, Blaine, Butler, In-
galls, Platt, and Farley.   More than one President has
approved the· suggestion, as, for example, President
Taft, who even urged a similar measure upon the attention of Congress in his annual message of 1912.
And it is significant that President Wilson has revived
the custom, in abeyance since Washington's time, of
delivering his communications to Congress in person,
at the Capitol, with his own voice, though no one has
had the temerity of attempting to subject him, on such
occasions, to interrogation.   The problem and its proposed solution have recently been stated by President
Nicholas Murray Butler of Columbia University in the
following terms:

"The business of national government has become so
huge and so complex that the sharp separation of the ex-

ecutive and the legislative powers to which we have been accustomed for one hundred and forty years is now distinctly disadvantageous. It brings in its train lack of coherence and of continuity in public policy; it conceals from the people much that they should know; and it prevents effective and quick co-operation between the Congress and the executive departments, both in times of emergency and in the conduct of the ordinary business of government. There is a way to overcome these embarrassments and difficulties without in any way altering the form of our government or breaking down the wise safeguards which the Constitution contains. That is to provide by law, as may be done very simply, that the members of the cabinet shall be entitled to occupy seats on the floor of the Senate and House of Representatives, with the right to participate in debate on matters relating to the business of their several departments, under such rules as the Senate and House respectively may prescribe. Such an act should further provide that the members of the cabinet *must* attend sessions of the Senate and House of Representatives at designated times, in order to give information asked by resolution or to reply to questions which may be propounded to them under the rules of the Senate and the House of Representatives."[1]

That this could be effected without a constitutional amendment is of course apparent. It rests with Congress. That body, by a line of precedents reaching back almost to the organization of the government, has established its power to require members of the cabinet to report directly to it on matters connected with their departmental affairs, and also its power to admit any person, in its discretion, to the floor of either house for the purpose of addressing it. It could scarcely be denied, then, that Congress might re-

[1] "A Program of Constructive Progress," an Address before the Commercial Club of St. Louis, February 16, 1918, reprinted in pamphlet form.

quire the cabinet ministers to render their reports and
to respond to questions on the floor of the house, in
person, and orally, or that it could afford them a standing right of access to either or both houses and a continuous privilege of addressing them from the floor on
subjects within their several provinces. Besides, as
President Taft pointed out, there is nothing in the
Constitution which explicitly authorizes Congress to
seat delegates from the territories in the House, with
the privilege of being heard in debate. Yet this has
been done, and there is no constitutional reason why
the same course might not be taken with respect to
members of the cabinet.

Though untried in the United States, this form of
participation by the executive officers in the work of
the legislature is familiar in several countries of Europe and of Latin-America; and it is to their experience, therefore, that we must turn for information as
to the advantages or disadvantages of the system. But
there is an important distinction to be kept in mind.
It has not been proposed that the members of the
American cabinet should be elected members of either
house of Congress, or that the President should select
the heads of departments from among the Senators or
Representatives. Indeed, the Constitution expressly
forbids this. But in several foreign countries the
ministers of state necessarily are (or they may be)
members of the legislative body, of course with the
right to vote. This necessarily imposes a multiple responsibility upon an official acting in this dual capacity,
first to his associates in the ministry, who must not, by
reason of anything he does, be exposed to the hazard

of losing the confidence of the house, then to his constituents at the polls, and finally to the legislative assembly itself, since parliamentary practice (at least in France, and probably elsewhere) requires the resignation of a minister upon the defeat of a measure which he has sponsored. But an American cabinet minister, given a seat in Congress with the right to introduce bills and argue for their enactment, would be under no responsibility whatever except that which always rests upon him, namely, responsibility to his chief, the President, and if the defeat of even his most earnestly desired measure, by even the most overwhelming majority, should bring about his resignation, it would be prompted by chagrin and not by the rules of the parliamentary game. If, therefore, the entrance of ministers into the processes of legislation produces beneficial results in England or in France, that is no argument whatever for the introduction of the system in the United States.

In England, it is a part of the unwritten constitution that every member of the cabinet must have a seat either in the House of Commons or the House of Lords, or in other words that the cabinet must be made up from among the members of the majority party in Parliament.

"The reason commonly given for such a limitation in the selection of ministers is that otherwise they could not be made responsible to Parliament, where they must be present in order to answer questions and give information relating to their departments. From the standpoint of Parliament this is perfectly true, but the converse is also true. The head of a department sits in the House of Commons quite as much in order to control the House as in order that the House may control him."[2]

In France, by article 6 of the Constitution of 1875,

"the ministers shall have entrance to both chambers, and shall be heard when they request it. They may be assisted, for the discussion of a specific bill, by commissioners named by decree of the President of the Republic."

In Switzerland, by article 101 of the Constitution of 1874,

"the members of the Federal Council shall have the right to speak, but not to vote, in both houses of the Federal Assembly, and also the right to make motions on the subject under consideration."

In Holland,

"the heads of the ministerial departments shall have seats in both houses. They shall have only a deliberative voice, unless they have been elected members of the house in which they sit. They shall furnish the houses, orally or in writing, such information as is requested, and the furnishing of which is not considered detrimental to the interests of the state. They may be summoned by either of the two houses to attend its meetings for this purpose." (Constitution of 1887, art. 94.)

In Norway, by the Constitution of 1814, article 74,

"the ministers of state and the councillors of state shall have the right to attend in the Storthing and in both branches thereof, and, upon an equality with its members, but without vote, to take part in the proceedings in so far as they are conducted publicly, but in secret sessions only in so far as the body in question may grant permission."

The Constitution of the "Confederate States of America" also provided:

[2] A. Lawrence Lowell, "The Government of England," Vol. I, p. 61.

"Congress may by law grant to the principal officer in each of the executive departments a seat upon the floor of either house, with the privilege of discussing any measure appertaining to his department."

In Belgium, Italy, and Spain, the ministers or secretaries of state are not necessarily members of either house of the legislature, but they may be so. If members, they have of course the right to vote, but otherwise not. In either case they have the entrance to both houses, and shall be heard upon their request.

The countries of Central and South America have generally followed the "presidential system" in so far as that ministers of state cannot at the same time be members of the legislative body. This is true in Brazil, Bolivia, Panama, Honduras, Mexico, the Argentine, Guatemala, Salvador, Nicaragua, Costa Rica, the Dominican Republic, Cuba, Peru, Ecuador, Colombia, and Paraguay. However, a notable exception is found in the case of Chile. But at the same time these countries have so far adopted the parliamentary system that the ministers have access to the floor of the legislature to explain and defend measures, or may be summoned there for that purpose. This is the constitutional rule, for example, in Bolivia, Panama, Chile, Paraguay, Honduras, Venezuela, Salvador, Nicaragua, Costa Rica, the Dominican Republic, Haiti, Peru, and Ecuador. For instance, the provisions of the Argentine constitution (articles 63, 90, and 92) are that

"each chamber shall have power to summon to its presence the members of the cabinet, in order that they may give orally the information which may be deemed necessary. As soon as Congress meets, each minister shall submit to it a report on the state of the nation so far as relates to the business of his own department. The ministers may attend the sessions of Congress and take part in the debates, but they shall have no vote."

In Colombia, the function of the ministers is still more sharply defined, and they are expressly made the connecting link between the executive and legislative departments. The 134th article of the constitution of that state provides:

"The ministers are the organs of communication between the executive and Congress. They may introduce bills in both houses, take part in the debates, and advise the President to approve or object to the acts of the legislature."

In Bolivia, the constitution not only permits but requires the participation of ministers in debate when the bill under discussion has been proposed by the executive. The 65th article is as follows:

"Laws may originate in the Senate or the Chamber of Deputies by bills introduced by their members, or by a message directed to them by the President of the Republic, on condition (in the latter case) that the bill shall be supported in the debates by at least one of the cabinet ministers, but he shall not have a vote."

On the other hand, the new constitution of Mexico (1917) adheres more closely to the practice prevailing in the United States. It is provided (article 93) that

"the secretaries of executive departments shall on the opening of each regular session report to the Congress as to the state of their respective departments. Either house may summon a secretary of an executive department to inform it, whenever a bill or other matter pertaining to his department is under discussion."

Sole among these countries Brazil seems anxious to exclude all vestiges of the parliamentary or cabinet system; for its constitution (article 51) declares that "the cabinet ministers shall *not* appear at the meetings of the Congress, and shall communicate with it only in writing, or personally in conferences with the committees of the chambers."

A very important part of the argument in favor of admitting the heads of departments to the floor of Congress is that it would enable them, promptly and viva voce, to furnish authoritative information on the needs and the workings of their departments and to explain and defend their own bills or those known to be administration measures. It will be of advantage, therefore, to see how the practice of parliamentary interrogation operates in those countries where it is in vogue. Turning first to England, we find a very complete account of the matter in President Lowell's important work on "The Government of England."[3]

"Isolated examples of questions addressed to ministers," he says, "can be found far back in the eighteenth century, but the habit did not become common until about sixty years ago. At that period, 100 or more questions were asked in the course of a session, and the first regulations were made regarding the time and method of putting them. Thereafter the practice grew so fast that in the seventies over 1000 were asked in a session, and by the end of the century it had increased to about 5000. In form, questions are simply requests for information. They must contain no argument, no statement of fact not needed to make their purport clear, and they must be addressed to that minister in the House in whose province the subject-matter of the inquiry falls. They cover almost every conceivable field; the intentions of ministers in the conduct of the business of the House; acts done by officials of all grades in every department of the public service; and even events that might be expected to give rise to action by the government. The process of answering questions gives to the Treasury Bench an air of omni-

[3] Vol. I, pp. 331-333.

science not wholly deserved, for notice of the question to be asked is sent in a day or two in advance, so as to give time for the permanent subordinates to hunt up the matter and supply their chief with the facts required. Questions are asked from various motives; sometimes simply to obtain information; sometimes to show to constituents the assiduity of their member, or to exhibit his opinions; sometimes to draw public attention to a grievance; sometimes to embarrass the government or make a telling point; and at times a question is asked by a supporter of the minister in order to give him a chance to bring out a fact effectively. But whatever the personal motive may be, the system provides a method of dragging before the House any act or omission by the departments of state, and of turning a searchlight upon every corner of the public service. The privilege is easily abused, but it helps very much to keep the administration of the country up to the mark, and it is a great safeguard against negligent or arbitrary conduct, or the growth of that bureaucratic arrogance which is quite unknown in England. The minister is not, of course, obliged to answer, but unless he can plead an obvious reason of public policy why he should not do so, as is often the case in foreign affairs, a refusal would look like an attempt to conceal, and would have a bad effect. Now while questions furnish a most effective means of bringing administrative errors to the notice of the House, they afford no opportunity for passing judgment upon them, and thereby they avoid the dangers of the French custom of interpellations. A question in England is not even followed by a debate. Often, indeed, the member says that his inquiry has not been fully answered, or interjects a remark, objection, or further question; but this is never allowed to grow into a discussion, and when the habit of asking supplementary questions becomes too common, the ministers refuse to answer them altogether, to the temporary exasperation of the opposition, or the Speaker himself checks them, enforcing the rule against introducing matter of argument. If no debate is in order, neither is a vote; and hence questions furnish a means of drawing public attention to an act, but not for collective censure of it by the House."

POWER TO LEGISLATION

In France, the interrogation of ministers plays a
much more important part in parliamentary tactics and
even in the administration of government, since an interpellation may be made the foundation of a motion
involving the question of the minister's continued re-
tention of the confidence of the house or his loss of
it, with the ultimate necessity of the tender of his
resignation, or even that of the entire ministry, if defeated. The present President of the French Republic
has thus explained the matter:

"The constitutional law of July 16, 1875, enacts in article 6: 'The ministers have the right of entry in the
two chambers and must be heard when they demand a
hearing.' Thus a minister who is a Senator may speak in
the Chamber of Deputies; a minister who is a Deputy
may ascend the tribune in the Senate; and a minister who
is neither a Senator nor Deputy can be heard in either
chamber. Ministers therefore intervene in the work of
legislation. They support the projects of laws which
they have introduced; they give their advice as to proposals initiated by Parliament; they oppose resolutions
and amendments of which they do not approve. As it
would be difficult for them to have cognizance of all the
matters in debate, they may be assisted by administrative
delegates appointed for the discussion of any particular
law projected, by decree of the President of the Republic. These auxiliaries are known as commissaries of
the government. Ministers, being responsible to the
chambers, may be questioned or interpellated upon the
acts of their administration. When a question is put to
a minister, he is free to reject it and to give no reply; but
he has not the right to evade an interpellation put in
writing by the President of the Assembly. The most that
he can do is to demand an adjournment of the discussion.
An interpellation in respect of internal policies is never
adjourned for more than a month. The Deputy who
brings forward the interpellation develops it, and the
other members of the Assembly take part in the debate if

they think fit, and the matter ends with the proposal of a parliamentary resolution, which is known as an 'order of the day.' 'The Chamber, making note of the declaration of the government,' or 'counting upon the government to . . .' or 'confiding in the government. . . .' If an order of the day in conformity with the desire of the interpellated minister is not adopted, the minister is defeated; he retires, and offers his resignation to the President of Council. If the interpellation involves the general policy of the cabinet, and the order of the day is unfavorable, the entire ministry is under the moral obligation of resigning."[4]

Could this system be adapted to the work of legislation in the United States? Let it be supposed that the members of the cabinet have been accorded the right to go upon the floor of Congress, to introduce bills, and to speak in their behalf. Then let it be supposed that a cabinet minister presents a bill relating to the military establishment (for the sake of example, a bill to raise an army by voluntary enlistment), but it develops in the course of interpellation and debate that both of the houses, by a strong but not overwhelming majority, are opposed to his ideas and would favor a conscription act. In England or Canada the matter would be pressed to a vote; in France an "order of the day" would be passed; in either case a situation would be created in which it would be incumbent on that minister to resign, and perhaps his fall would involve that of the entire ministry. But not only that would result. The next step would be the appointment of a ministry in sympathy with the views of the parliamentary majority, and they would frame, introduce, and carry a different bill on the same subject. And

4 Raymond Poincaré, "How France is Governed," pp. 200-202.

thus the will of the majority would be accomplished. Not so, however, in the United States. The defeated minister would not resign unless he found himself in disagreement with the President. That is a case which has rarely occurred in our history. Otherwise the situation would result in a deadlock, the majority not being able to effect its will unless numerically strong enough to overcome the President's probable veto; or else the President would be able to break down opposition by influence, pressure, promises, and other devices of the lobby, and so thwart the real desire of the majority. We return, then, to the conclusion already indicated, that it is not feasible to have a parliamentary system of government, even to the extent proposed, without ministerial responsibility.

It is argued, and with some justice, that the proposed change in the relation of the cabinet to the Congress would obviate the necessity of whispered interviews in the corridors and cloak rooms, bring into the open many proceedings which are now too often of a subterranean character, and place the heads of departments in an attitude towards legislation at once correct and befitting their high station. Nicholas Murray Butler, in the pamphlet already cited, says:

"A cabinet officer is in a much more dignified position if he is permitted to answer questions as to his official conduct and business on the floor of a legislative body, and to make his reply part of the public record, than if he is interrogated in a committee room as an incident in some general inquiry."

This suggests, what is indeed the fact, that the problem is wide enough to involve a consideration of the powers and procedure of the standing committees. In substance, the proposal is to take the cabinet minister out of the committee room and place him on the floor of the house. A French writer on comparative constitutional law, after speaking of the standing committees of the Senate and House as "organs of relation" between the legislative and executive powers, has said:

"Ministers who wish to have a bill introduced confer with the chairman of the appropriate committee. Some of these committees exercise by this means an incessant supervision over the administration. They cite the ministers before them and interrogate them concerning their methods and objects. This supervision is contrary to the principle of the separation of powers; it is secret, and consequently favors intrigues and compromises, and may hinder the progress of the government. The result is disorder and impotence."[5]

On this, however, it is necessary to remark that such examinations are now very seldom private or confidential, except where important military secrets are involved or delicate affairs of state. Almost always a member of the cabinet presents himself before a committee, whether on summons or at his own request, for the purpose of a public hearing, at which he has full opportunity not only to supply information but also to press his own views and arguments, and the proceedings are published at large and in detail in the press. The argument for publicity and for placing the heads of departments in a correct attitude towards legislation would therefore appear to have little weight in so far as it relates to discussion of the policies of law-making

[5] Esmein, "Éléments de Droit constitutional et comparée," (Paris, 1914), as quoted by Miñana, "La Division de los Poderes del Estado," p. 216.

or the presentation of information for the guidance of the legislators; but it must be admitted that it does not lack force in its relation to the more or less stealthy and certainly undignified exertion of pressure by executive officers to secure the success or defeat, the moulding or the modification, of pending bills, always assuming that such practices cannot otherwise be brought to an end.

Those who favor the admission of the members of the cabinet to the floor of the houses, with the right to participate in debate, believe that, under such conditions, the executive departments would be presided over by men of much higher intelligence and greater capacity. Thus, ex-Governor McCall (in a published interview already quoted) says:

"One effect of such a change would be an improvement in the average capacity of cabinet members. We have had members appointed to the cabinet who have had little or no experience in public affairs or in maintaining their views before a parliamentary body. I think men would be required in the cabinet of a very different calibre from some of those who have heretofore been put at the head of a department of the government, should some change along this line be made."

In the report of the Senate committee on this subject, to which reference has been made, it was said:

"This system will require the selection of the strongest men to be heads of departments, and will require them to be well equipped with the knowledge of their offices. It will also require the strongest men to be the leaders of Congress and participate in debate. It will bring these strong men in contact, perhaps in conflict, to advance the public weal, and thus stimulate their abilities and their efforts, and will thus assuredly result to the good of the country."

President Taft, who strongly favored the proposed change, has recorded his belief that

"this would impose on the President greater difficulty in selecting his cabinet, and would lead him to prefer men of legislative experience who have shown their power to take care of themselves in legislative debate. It would stimulate the head of each department by the fear of public and direct inquiry into a more thorough familiarity with the actual operations of his department and into a closer supervision of its business."[6]

To the same effect also is the opinion of Dr. Butler, who observes:

"Were such a custom to be established, an almost certain result would be the selection as heads of the great executive departments of men of large ability and personal force, men able to explain and defend their policies and measures before the Congress of the United States in the face of the whole country."[7]

But all this is predicated upon the supposition that an incoming President has a perfectly free hand in selecting the members of his cabinet, and could choose them with regard solely to their ability and experience. But has this ideal ever been realized in our history? In fact, cabinet appointments are often dictated by considerations of political expedience. There are powerful and dangerous rivals to be placated or disarmed. There are party leaders, campaign managers, heavy contributors to the campaign funds, whose preferences must be consulted, whether they lie in the direction of personal ambition or the distribution of high offices. Good party policy also requires a certain geographical apportionment of the cabinet ministers. And is it al-

[6] William H. Taft, "Our Chief Magistrate," p. 31.
[7] "A Program of Constructive Progress," ut supra.

ways certain that a President, himself ambitious and conscious of a gift for leadership, would be willing to invite into his official family, and to place on the floor of Congress as his spokesmen and representatives, men of very conspicuous and perhaps overshadowing ability? The trouble with most political formulas is that they leave out of view the personal element in the equation. But it was precisely this point—political power as a function of personality—that the founders of the Republic had in mind when they framed the Constitution and devised the form of government under which we have hitherto prospered.

Minor arguments are not wanting for the suggested change in the status of the heads of departments. Thus, it is said that, with the best intentions in the world, Congress often blunders sadly in its enactments for the lack of exact information upon specific details, and that this would not happen if the cabinet minister possessing precisely the needed facts and figures were present in debate, and if it were his duty either to volunteer or to supply on request what the legislators should learn. President Taft says that the proposed new system

"would give the President what he ought to have, some direct initiative in legislation and an opportunity, through the presence of his competent representatives in Congress, to keep each house advised of the facts in the actual operation of the government. The time lost in Congress over useless discussion of issues that might be disposed of by a single statement from the head of a department, no one can appreciate unless he has filled such a place."[8]

And in the same strain it is remarked by Dr. Butler:

[8] William H. Taft, "Our Chief Magistrate," p. 31.

"Had such a provision been in force during the past generation, the nation would have been spared many an unhappy and misleading controversy. What has sometimes been made public only after the labor and cost of an elaborate investigation by committee, might have been had without delay through the medium of questions put to a cabinet officer on the floor of the Senate or the House of Representatives." "No feature of British parliamentary practice," he adds, "is more useful or contributes more to a public understanding of what the executive is doing, than the proceedings at question-time in the House of Commons."[9]

Again, it is said that, at his place on the floor of Congress, a member of the cabinet would stand as the spokesman of the administration, and by explaining clearly and with authority the attitude of the President towards a pending bill, or his wishes in regard to contemplated legislation, he would be able to avoid disastrous misunderstandings and possible vetoes. But in fact, no one of our recent Presidents has hesitated for a moment to tell Congress what was his attitude towards any pending bill or to express in concrete form his views as to expedient legislation. Nor have Presidents hesitated to employ cabinet ministers as their spokesmen in these matters.

It has been objected that the new duties sought to be imposed upon the members of the cabinet, with reference to their attendance upon the houses of Congress and the introduction and engineering of legislation, would absorb so much of their time and attention that they would be unable properly to conduct the ordinary administration of their departments. This seems highly probable. But a remedy was suggested

[9] "A Program of Constructive Progress," ut supra.

by the Senate committee appointed in 1881 to consider the question, in their report to which reference has already been made, as follows:

"If it should appear by actual experience that the heads of departments in fact have not time to perform the additional duty imposed on them by this bill, the force of their offices should be increased or the duties devolving on them personally should be diminished. An under-secretary should be appointed, to whom could be confided that routine of administration which requires only order and accuracy. The principal officers could then confine their attention to those duties which require wise discretion and intellectual activity. Thus they would have abundance of time for their duties under this bill. Indeed, your committee believes that the public interest would be subserved if the secretaries were relieved of the harrassing cares of distributing clerkships and closely supervising the mere machinery of the departments. Your committee believes that the adoption of this bill and the effective execution of its provisions will be the first step toward a sound civil-service reform which will secure a larger wisdom in the adoption of policies and a better system in their execution."

A little reflection will show that this proposal involves a profound change in our system of administration, and notwithstanding the eminence of the names signed to the committee's report, the opinion may be hazarded that it would be very difficult to get the consent of the American people to intrust the conduct of their public business to a hierarchy of under-secretaries possessing a genius for "order and accuracy," but not required to exhibit "intellectual activity." Under such a regime, the under-secretaries would inevitably tend to become permanent officials. Their very efficiency would be an argument against their removal upon a change of administration. And hence it would sometimes happen that the actual government of the great executive departments would be in the hands of men not in sympathy with their political chiefs or with the President's closest advisers. Anyone who realizes the important part now played by the assistant secretaries of the several departments will perceive that such a system would lead only to incessant jealousy and conflict within the department or else to stagnation and decay in the public business.

To sum up the argument, the proposal to bestow upon the members of the cabinet the right of initiative in legislation and the right to take part in the debates of Congress appears a very simple matter. But who can foretell the consequences to which it might lead? Very wise were the words of Lord Bryce, written now thirty years ago but closely applicable to present-day conditions.

"While some bid England borrow from her daughter, other Americans conceive that the separation of the legislature from the executive has been carried too far in the United States, and suggest that it would be an improvement if the ministers of the President were permitted to appear in both houses of Congress to answer questions, perhaps even to join in debate. I have no space to discuss the merits of this proposal, but must observe that it might lead to changes more extensive than its advocates seem to contemplate. The more the President's ministers come into contact with Congress, the more difficult will it be to maintain the independence of Congress which he and they now possess. When not long ago the Norwegian Storthing forced the king of Sweden and Norway to consent to his ministers appearing in that legislature, the king, perceiving the import of the concession, resolved to choose in future ministers in accord with the party holding a majority in the Storthing. It is hard to say, when one begins to make alterations in an old house, how far one will be led on in rebuilding, and I doubt whether this change in the present American system, possibly in itself desirable, might not be found to involve a reconstruction large enough to put a new face upon several parts of that system."[10]

No clear prevision of the renovations ultimately to be effected is of course possible. But if, as Bryce thought, the change might lead to struggles on the part of the executive to maintain its independence of Congress, the opinion is at least defensible that the reaction might be in the other direction, that is, in the way of increasing the dominance of the executive over the legislative branch. Few lessons on this point are to be drawn from our previous history. But such as they are, they are instructive. It will be recalled that Washington once visited the Senate, accompanied by the Secretary of War, General Knox, for the purpose of obtaining the "advice and consent" of the Senate on certain matters connected with the negotiation of a treaty. The seven propositions submitted were so framed that they could all be answered by a simple affirmative or negative. Knox had with him a paper containing an explanation of the matters in question, and Washington expected that a vote (of course affirmative) would be taken immediately upon the reading of this paper. But instead, a motion was made to refer the matter to a committee. Upon this Washington started to his feet with every symptom of violent anger. "This defeats every purpose of my coming here," he exclaimed, and added that he had brought the Secretary of War with him to give every necessary information; that the Secretary knew all about

[10] Bryce, "American Commonwealth" (1889), Vol. I, p. 284.

the business, and yet he was delayed and could not go on with the matter. But after a little, the President, though professing not to understand the necessity for the intervention of a committee, observed that he had no objection to postponing the matter to a day fixed in the near future. Senator Maclay (in whose "Journal" the incident is recorded) continues thus:

"A pause for some time ensued. We waited for him to withdraw. He did so with a discontented air. Had it been any other man than the man whom I wish to regard as the first character in the world, I would have said, with sullen dignity. I cannot now be mistaken. The President wishes to tread on the necks of the Senate. Commitment will bring the matter to discussion, at least in the committee, where he is not present. He wishes us to see with the eyes and hear with the ears of his Secretary only; the Secretary to advance the premises, the President to draw the conclusions, and to bear down our deliberations with his personal authority and presence. Form only will be left to us." But he added: "This will soon cure itself."

V

THE SELECTIVE OR PARTIAL VETO

When an appropriation bill is passed by the two houses of Congress and laid before the President, he often finds strong grounds for disapproving some one or more of its various items, or perhaps an irrelevant "rider" attached to it, while he is entirely in favor of the rest. Yet he must deal with the bill as a whole. He must either sign it or return it with his objections to the house in which it originated. The veto power given by the Constitution is not selective. That it should be made so—that the President should be given at least a suspensive veto as to items selected from perhaps a large number included in a bill without the necessity of condemning the whole—has been very frequently proposed in Congress. It is said that at as many as forty-five different times resolutions for the amendment of the Constitution in this particular have been offered. The matter has been urged by several of the Presidents, notably by Grant and Arthur, in their messages to Congress. President Grant, in his fifth annual message, December 1, 1873, recommended to Congress a constitutional amendment

"to authorize the executive to approve of so much of any measure passed by the two houses of Congress as his judgment may dictate, without approving the whole, the disapproved portion or portions to be subjected to the same rules as now, to wit, to be referred back to the house in which the measure or measures originated, and, if passed by a two-thirds vote of both houses, then to become a law without the approval of the President. I would add to this a provision that there should not be legislation by Congress during the last twenty-four hours of its sitting, except upon vetoes, in order to give the executive an opportunity to examine and approve or disapprove bills understandingly." He thought that this "would protect the public against the many abuses and waste of public moneys which creep into appropriation bills and other important measures passed during the expiring hours of Congress, to which otherwise due consideration cannot be given."

President Arthur, in his second annual message, December 4, 1882, objected to the practice of grouping large numbers of items of appropriations in the general river and harbor bill. This practice, he said,

"inevitably tends to secure the success of the bill as a whole, though many of the items, if separately considered, could scarcely fail of rejection."

He urged the enactment of a separate bill for each such item, but if this was impracticable, he called attention to the fact that the constitutions of fourteen states (at that time) permitted the executive to veto separate items in appropriation bills, and said:

"I commend to your careful consideration the question whether an amendment of the federal Constitution in the particular indicated would not afford the best remedy for what is often grave embarrassment both to members of Congress and to the executive, and is sometimes a serious public mischief."

Arthur was so convinced of the necessity of such an amendment that, although no result followed his recommendation, he renewed it in his third and fourth annual messages.

Moreover, this proposed change has been discussed

with very general approbation in the public press, and
has been advocated by large and influential civic bodies
and associations of business men. Yet the movement
has hitherto failed to enlist that united and determined
popular insistence which is still required for effecting
a change in the organic law. It may be that it will
eventually succeed. But if so, it will come, as constitutional amendments should come, not as the fruit of
sudden impulse, but as the result of a sound and natural growth in our political institutions.

Executive authority to veto separate items in appropriation bills first appears in the constitution of the
Confederate States, adopted in 1861. The same clause
was written into the constitutions of two or three of
the southern states during the reconstruction period,
and has met with such general favor on the part of the
states that it is now a part of the fundamental law of
no less than thirty-seven of them. That is to say, the
governor now possesses this authority in all of the
states except five of the New England states (Massachusetts having given her governor the right of partial
veto by constitutional amendment in 1918), North
Carolina (where he has no veto power at all), and a
group of five central or western states comprising In-
diana, Iowa, Nevada, Tennessee, and Wisconsin. It is
also a significant fact that Congress has extended this
power to the Governor of Porto Rico and the Governor-General of the Philippines in the recent acts providing for the civil government of those possessions.

That the purpose and operation of this selective veto
may be made clear, it will be appropriate to quote here
the provision of the Constitution of New York on the

subject, which may be taken as typical of the rest. It is as follows:

"If any bill presented to the governor contain several items of appropriation of money, he may object to one or more of such items, while approving of the other portion of the bill. In such case, he shall append to the bill, at the time of signing it, a statement of the items to which he objects, and the appropriation so objected to shall not take effect. If the legislature be in session, he shall transmit to the house in which the bill originated a copy of such statement, and the items objected to shall be separately considered. If on reconsideration one or more of such items be approved by two-thirds of the members elected to each house, the same shall be part of the law, notwithstanding the objections of the governor."

Some state governors, including ex-Governor Whitman of New York, have strongly urged upon the state legislatures the submission of a constitutional amendment which would permit the executive not only to "object" to particular items, but to "reduce" those deemed excessive. And in Massachusetts this has been accomplished by an amendment adopted in 1918, which provides that "the governor may disapprove or reduce items or parts of items in any bill appropriating money." This seems a logical extension of the power already granted. For it might well happen that an appropriation for a particular public object might be not only commendable but even necessary for the efficient conduct of government, and yet a governor, exercising his conscientious judgment on the subject, might consider it grossly excessive. But legislatures hesitate at this point. To enlarge the governor's power in this respect seems too complete a surrender of the control of the purse, which historically does not belong to the

executive branch.   Yet the governors of several other
states have claimed that their constitutional authority
to "disapprove" items in appropriation bills included
the right to reduce those objected to in amount.   The
governor of Pennsylvania has more than once acted on
this assumption, and he has been sustained by a decision of the Supreme Court of that state.   In four or
five other states the same course has been taken by the
executive, but the courts have not yet passed upon its
legality.   In Colorado, in view of the fact that the legislature is prohibited from making appropriations in ex-
cess of the amount provided for by tax laws then in
existence or enacted for the purpose, the Supreme
Court of that state says that the clause in the constitution giving this power to the governor

"shows a clear purpose to invest the executive with discretion to save such appropriations as are necessary to
defray the expenses of the government, without the danger of incumbering or defeating them by excessive or im-
provident expenditures."

In Illinois and Mississippi, however, the courts have
ruled that the power given to the governor to veto any
distinct item or section in an appropriation bill does
not give him authority to disapprove of a part of a
distinct item and approve the remainder, and if he
vetoes a part of an item, as by striking out the words
"per annum" or by approving part of an item and disapproving the remainder, his action is void.   And in
Oklahoma it has been decided that when an appropriation bill contains only a single item, the governor cannot approve the appropriation and the amount of it and
at the same time disapprove the parts of the act which

direct how the appropriated funds shall be apportioned.

But if the governor is to be permitted to exercise the veto power upon separate portions of a bill, why stop at appropriation bills? South Carolina and Washington authorize their governors to veto any section of any bill presented to them. In Alabama, the constitution authorizes the governor to return a bill to the legislature without his approval, but with a message proposing amendments "which would remove his objections." If both houses accept the amendments, the bill is then returned to the governor to be acted on as in other cases. If either rejects the amendments, it must reconsider the bill. If both reject the amendments by a majority of the whole number of members elected to each house, the bill becomes a law. In Massachusetts, it is the privilege of the governor, within five days after any bill shall have been laid before him, to return it to that branch of the legislature in which it originated, with a recommendation that any amendment or amendments specified by him be made therein. So also in Australia,

"the Governor-General may return to the house in which it originated any proposed law so presented to him, and may transmit therewith any amendments which he may recommend, and the houses may deal with the recommendation."

In Virginia, if the governor

"approves the general purpose of any bill, but disapproves any part or parts thereof, he may return it, with recommendations for its amendment, to the house in which it originated, whereupon the same proceedings shall be had in both houses upon the bill and his recommendations in relation to its amendment as is above provided in relation to a bill which he shall have returned without his approval and with his objections thereto; provided that if, after such reconsideration, both houses, by a vote of a majority of the members present in each, shall agree to amend the bill in accordance with his recommendation in relation thereto, or either house by such vote shall fail or refuse to so amend it, then, and in either case, the bill shall be again sent to him, and he may act upon it as if it were then before him for the first time."

And this enlarged participation of the executive in the business of making the laws, either by the selective veto or by the offering of amendments, is familiar in the countries of Latin-America, not only in practice but by the specific authorization of their constitutions. In Mexico, the Argentine, Paraguay, Colombia, and Panama, the president may veto any bill in whole or in part. In Ecuador and Costa Rica, his objections to any bill may take the form of corrections, modifications, or amendments. The constitutional provision in the last-named republic is quite interesting. It is as follows:

"The executive power may object to any bill, either because he judges it as a whole to be inadvisable or because he believes it necessary that it should be amended or reformed, and in the latter case he shall propose the changes to be made. . . . If the modifications [proposed by the executive] are adopted, the bill shall be sent to the executive power, which cannot in this case refuse its approval. If the amendments are rejected, and the two-thirds vote necessary to pass the bill is not secured, it shall be placed in the archives and cannot be considered again until the next ordinary session."

This system of permitting the executive authority to point out defects in a bill or make suggestions for its emendation, without being under the necessity of undoing the entire work of the legislature upon it by his veto, has been explained and defended by a former governor of Alabama in a paper recently published, from which the following quotations are taken:

"In Alabama the power to veto has been accompanied with the power to amend, a power which we believe is not granted to the executive under the terms of the constitution of any other state, except in a modified form in the state of Virginia, where the governor is permitted to suggest, but not to initiate, amendments. In the exercise of this prerogative in Alabama, the governor may return bills presented to him without giving his approval and may suggest and prepare amendments which would remove his objections. These amendments the legislature may concur in, or, not concurring, it may proceed to pass the bill over the veto, as in cases where the power to amend is not given.

"This power of amendment, while a new idea in our theory of government, has proved to be of great value. By its exercise the governor has been enabled in many instances to amend a meritorious statute, otherwise unconstitutional, so as to give it validity, or to suggest and submit additions or call attention to omissions which would better adapt the proposed law to the conditions it was designed to meet. Nor is this power any undue extension of the executive function. If the governor is properly a part of the law-making power to the extent of approving or disapproving bills or initiating legislation by submitting his recommendations in the form of bills, if the public is entitled to his judgment on the laws affecting it, it is an illogical limitation on that duty to restrain it within the narrow channels of approval or disapproval of a bill as it stands, when, with the elimination of unwise provisions or the addition of needed sections, it could be easily altered into fitness to serve a beneficial purpose.

"But it may be claimed that by conferring on the governor the veto power vested in him by the Alabama constitution we would be delegating to him legislative functions. It is well, however, to remember that the capacity of a law to serve the purposes for which it is designed cannot be fully known until it is put into operation. It is in the execution of laws that their defects become apparent. The executive has, therefore, a practical experience in which members of the legislature are frequently and of necessity wanting, which peculiarly qualifies him to point out the parts in which a proposed law is insufficient, onerous, or ill-considered, and to remove by his amendment those features which bear too heavily on rights which should not be burdened or impaired, or to add those without which the act would be ill-balanced, ineffective, or incapable of practical or proper enforcement. Hence it is apparent that the power to amend a bill as provided in the Alabama constitution is intimately related to the executive function, and only gives the people the benefit of the knowledge which a governor acquires by the exercise of the duties of the chief executive office.''[1]

Sound reasons for granting a partial or discriminative veto to the President of the United States, in respect to money bills, are not far to seek. Our whole wasteful and haphazard method of making appropriations is at fault. "Pork-barrel" legislation is a notorious and malodorous fact. So also is the pernicious habit of attaching "riders" to appropriation bills, often totally unrelated to the general subject, and which would surely incur the executive disapproval if presented separately. Arguing for a constitutional amendment to counteract these tendencies, a respectable newspaper has recently observed:

"One of the great evils of legislation, state and national, lies in the fact that vicious items find their way into appropriation bills, and remain there because the executive must take his choice between vetoing a bill generally meritorious or necessary for the operation of government affairs, or accepting it despite its bad features.

[1] Hon. Emmet O'Neal, "Strengthening the Power of the Executive," in *Virginia Law Review*, December, 1917, pp. 163-165.

The public buildings bill, the river and harbors bill, and similar other measures, ordinarily contain many articles of merit along with others of no merit, which are put there as a sop to members whose votes are needed to pass the legislation, or at the behest of members who are anxious to get something out of the public treasury for their districts. The President cannot approve the good features of the bill and strike out the bad, but must approve the whole or veto it. Under the proposed amendment a President could approve a bill in principle and strike out its objectionable features. Hardly anyone will quarrel with the wisdom of a policy which will permit of the exercise of such discretion. Then there is the habit of attaching riders to appropriation bills as a means of jamming legislation through. A matter may have no more bearing on the bill to which it is attached as a rider than the canals of Mars have with the price of eggs, but it is attached and passed, and when the measure comes before the executive he has his choice between signing the bill, rider and all, or vetoing some appropriation measure whose passage is essential."

Furthermore, bills for raising revenue might often be more acceptable to the country at large if subject to executive revision item by item. At least the possession of such a power by the President would do away with the unseemly spectacle (witnessed in some former administrations) of bargaining in progress over a tariff or revenue bill between the White House and the Capitol.

But on the other hand, do we seriously wish to add anything to the transcendent powers already possessed by the President? Leaving wholly aside the special exigencies created by the recent war, and considering only the facts as recorded in the preceding pages of this volume, it is not too much to say that the presidency has grown into an office of such predominant

influence and tremendous power as would utterly have
appalled the founders of the American democracy, and
such as were but dimly within the vision of even the
fathers of the present generation. Would it be wise,
would it be prudent, in view of all possible eventuali-
ties, to withdraw from Congress any remnant of its
fast diminishing control of the public interests?

Counsels of wisdom and prudence in this matter
have been expressed by one of our former Presidents,
to which it would be well to give heed.

"While for some purposes it would be useful for the
executive to have the power of partial veto, if we could
always be sure of its wise and conscientious exercise, I
am not entirely sure that it would be a safe provision.
It would greatly enlarge the influence of the President,
already large enough from patronage and party loyalty,
and other causes. I am inclined to think that it is better to trust to the action of the people in condemning the
party which becomes responsible for such riders than to
give, in such a powerful instrument like this, a temptation to its sinister use by a President eager for continued
political success. This use by Congress of riders upon
appropriation bills to force a President to consent to
legislation which he disapproves shows a spirit of destructive factionalism and a lack of a sense of responsibility for the maintenance of the government. If such a
sense of responsibility does not pervade all branches of
the government, executive, legislative, and judicial, the
government cannot remain a going concern. Instances of
abuse of this sort by Congress, therefore, must be regarded as exceptional, as indeed they are, and an effort
to remedy them by a change in constitutional provision
would be legislation intended to pump patriotism into
public officers by force. This method will certainly be
found futile if such patriotism and sense of responsibility do not exist without it. If it is urged that the President should have power to veto items in appropriation

bills to restrain legislative extravagance, the answer is
that this is not the best way.   The proper remedy for
that evil is the budget amendment."[2]

If we examine this question in the light of actual examples drawn from our legislative history, it will become apparent that the power of a selective veto would
be of no avail to a President who should be opposed
by a strong majority in Congress, that it is unnecessary to a President who has a decisive control over
Congress, and that it could possibly be useful only in
cases where the executive is in generally harmonious
relations with the legislature but does not lead or direct it.   For an instance of the first category, the army
appropriation bill of 1867 contained a rider providing
that the President's orders to the army should be given
only through the General of the Army, who could not
be removed from office without the previous approval
of the Senate.   This was intended to, and did, virtually depose the President from the exercise of his functions as commander in chief.   The bill also contained
a clause ordering the disbanding of the militia of all
the states lately in rebellion.   Both these provisions
were violently distasteful to Andrew Johnson, then
President.   But he could not veto them without de-
stroying the entire bill.   He knew that if he took that
course the obnoxious measures would sooner or later
be enacted over his veto.   But only two days remained
of the session.   Therefore he returned the bill with
his signature, but with a message that he approved it
only to save the appropriation and that he "protested"
against the riders.

[2] William H. Taft, "Our Chief Magistrate," p. 27.

But on the other hand, in the summer of 1918, within the space of two weeks, President Wilson vetoed no less than three of the great appropriation bills, in each case because of his objection to some particular item or provision, and yet the appropriations were not lost. This result followed from his powerful influence with Congress. On June 29th, he sent a message to the House refusing his approval of the annual post-office appropriation bill, because he objected to an item in it which made provision for continuing the pneumatic mail-tube system in certain of the large cities. It will be seen that, in order to express his disagreement with this one detail, he was obliged to veto the entire bill, although it was the act which was essential to the continuation of the entire postal service after July 1st. But what happened was that, after an ineffectual attempt to pass the bill over the veto, the committee reported a new bill to the House, which was absolutely identical with the former bill except for the omission of the item objected to, and this was passed without debate and without a roll call. And this was done on the very same day on which the veto message was received, and later in the day the Senate passed the amended bill. Again, on the 1st of July, the President vetoed the legislative, executive, and judicial appropriation bill. The reason was that he objected to the so-called "Borland amendment," which would have required the clerks in the governmental departments to work eight hours a day instead of seven, without an increase of pay. On the same day, the House, by a vote of 246 to 50, refused to override the President's veto, and on the following day, this great appropriation bill was passed, with the Borland amendment eliminated. On the 12th of July, the President vetoed the agricultural appropriation bill because of his objection to an item in it which fixed the price of wheat at $2.40 per bushel. On the following day it became apparent that the bill could not be passed over his veto, but further action on it was temporarily postponed because of the agreement of Congress at that time to take a recess.

Another view of the subject, but leading to the same conclusion, was presented by the Bureau of Municipal Research in its appraisal of the constitution and government of New York, prepared for submission to the constitutional convention of that state in 1915. Speaking of the provision allowing the governor to veto separate items in appropriation bills, it was said:

"Under such circumstances the governor is held responsible for the acceptance or reduction of items as passed in measures for which he is not responsible. The power operates as a check on an irresponsible legislature. It does not cure irresponsibility. It does not supply leadership. It does put into the hands of the governor the power to punish political enemies by using the pruning knife where he will, in the plea of economy. The power is not constructive, but may be made highly destructive. It transfers from the legislative committee room to the executive chamber all the pressure that has been brought to bear in furtherance of the plans of an irresponsible boss. It simply invites another dark-room proceeding, instead of having the business of the state done in the open, in the face of the opposition."

If the legislature is still in session when the governor acts on the bill,

"he may, if he chooses, get a fair statement of a consistent fiscal policy before the legislature for discussion and action. But usually the legislature has adjourned before the governor has an opportunity to act on many appropriations."

The Bureau thinks that a much better plan is that of a budget (not merely advisory but compulsory), under which the governor is required to formulate, submit, and defend the appropriation bills, thus

"securing economy and responsibility in the appropriation and management of public funds."

The question of enlarging the veto power should not be considered as an isolated problem. It is but an element, or a symptom, of that vigorous trend towards executive leadership which is so markedly developing in our political philosophy, and which, in respect to the science of government, many observers believe to be the most significant phenomenon of our times. The new program, as we have seen, involves supplementing the administrative and appointive powers of the executive branch by intrusting to it also both initiative and responsibility in the framing of the laws. It is a departure from the old theory that the guardianship of the public welfare was vested in the legislature. The new theory would confide it to the executive. The selective veto is a step in that direction.

VI

EXECUTIVE ORDERS AND DECREES

In all strong governments which have recognized
the division of powers, thus setting the executive over
against the legislative branch, it has been a part of the
struggle for supremacy between them that the executive should seek to obtain for itself a more or less extensive power of law-making independent of the legislative body; that is, a power to give to its ordinances,
by whatever name they may be called (orders, decrees,
regulations, or proclamations) the force of law in the
sense that they shall be imperative and that they shall
be enforceable by the courts, yet without the concurrence or previous authorization of the legislature. Almost everywhere this encroaching tendency has been
checked. Almost everywhere constitutional practice
has settled the rule that executive ordinances, when of
such a character as to affect the general public, are not
"laws" in this sense except when made in pursuance of
explicit constitutional or statutory authority. Lacking this sanction, they may indeed fall within the
proper scope of administrative action, but they serve
only the purpose of notice, warning, or exhortation,
and do not, like "laws" properly so called, restrain the
citizen from doing something otherwise lawful, or
force him into a course of conduct to which he was not
previously compelled. Yet, in the mind of a strong

and dominant executive officer, determined upon leadership, there must always be present the temptation to put a very liberal construction upon such regulation-making powers as are implicated in his constitutionally defined powers and prerogatives, and likewise to push to the limit and perhaps beyond it any authority delegated to him by the legislature for filling in the details of legislation on a given subject or carrying a statute into effect. And given a contest for leadership and control, this weapon in the hands of the executive is neither antiquated nor rusty. It is more powerful now than ever. And a study of its use and possibilities is of especial importance in its relation to the general subject of the growth of executive power, in view of the very marked and increasing tendency of legislative bodies, when dealing with subjects of broad general interest, to satisfy themselves with outlining a general plan or prescribing general principles in their statute, leaving the details of their enactments and all that concerns their practical operation to be governed by regulations made by the executive or administrative officers.

Before attempting a description of the President's existing authority in these matters, or a forecast of its possible future use, it will be well to survey the constitutional history and practice of some other countries, in order to see what lessons of experience or warning may be gleaned from them.

In England, long after the establishment of parliamentary government, many kings in succession chafed under the restraints which Parliament imposed upon them, and sought to recover the power of independent legislation claimed to have belonged to their predecessors. Not merely that English kings periodically asserted the right to suspend acts of Parliament, but they coveted the right to go their own way in the making of rules for the governance of the realm alongside of Parliament or without reference to it. They cast envious eyes upon the traditionary powers once ascribed to the King in Council, and sought to make ordinances and proclamations emanating from that source what they once had been, a real and living force. Henry VIII once caught Parliament in a subservient or complaisant mood. In 1539, an act was passed providing that

"the King for the time being, with the advice of his Council, or the more part of them, may set forth proclamations under such penalties and pains as to him and them shall seem necessary, which shall be observed as though they were made by Act of Parliament; but this shall not be prejudicial to any person's inheritance, offices, liberties, goods, chattels, or life; and whosoever shall willingly offend any article in the said proclamations shall pay such forfeitures, or be so long imprisoned, as shall be expressed in the said proclamations; and if any offending will depart the realm to the intent he will not answer his said offense, he shall be adjudged a traitor."

But this amazing piece of legislation was repealed in the reign of Edward VI. Dicey remarks:

"It is curious to notice how revolutionary would have been the results of the statute had it remained in force." One of them would have been that

"an English king would have become nearly as despotic as a French monarch."[1]

The same distinguished author, in his instructive description of the constitution of England, calls at-

[1] Dicey, "Law of the Constitution," p. 49.

tention to the distinction between "laws" properly so called, as being made by the legislature, and "ordinances" having the force of law though not in strictness laws, as being rather decrees of the executive power than acts of the legislature. He says:

"This distinction exists in one form or another in most continental states and is not without great practical utility. In foreign countries, the legislature generally confines itself to laying down general principles of legislation, and leaves them, with great advantage to the public, to be supplemented by decrees or regulations which are the work of the executive. The cumbersomeness and prolixity of English statute law is due in no small measure to futile endeavors of Parliament to work out the details of large legislative changes. The evil has become so apparent that in modern times acts of Parliament constantly contain provisions empowering the Privy Council, the judges, or some other body, to make rules under the act for the determination of details which cannot be settled by Parliament. But this is only an awkward mitigation of an acknowledged evil, and the substance no less than the form of the law would, it is probable, be a good deal improved if the executive government of England could like that of France, by means of decrees, ordinances, or proclamations having the force of law, work out the detailed application of the general principles embodied in the acts of the legislature."[2]

As a matter of fact both orders in council and proclamations enter into the texture of English statute law to a much greater degree than is apparent to those who think of Parliament as the only fount of law. Orders and proclamations differ in their formal style and language, but essentially they both emanate from the privy council and have exactly the same effect as law. An order in council is dated "At the Court at

[2] Dicey, op. cit., p. 49.

Buckingham Palace," on such a day, "Present, the
King's Most Excellent Majesty in Council," and recites that "His Majesty is pleased, by and with the advice of his privy council, to order, and it is hereby ordered, as follows," etc.   A royal proclamation is
headed: "By the King," and recites "we have thought
fit, by and with the advice of our privy council, to issue this our royal proclamation, and we do hereby
proclaim, direct, and ordain as follows," etc.   There
are a few exceptional cases in English law where an
order or proclamation may be made without previous
legislative sanction, as, for instance, where Parliament
is summoned by an executive proclamation.   But otherwise it is a firmly settled principle that the sphere of
executive legislation must be limited to those details
as to which the authority of Parliament has been specifically delegated.   Without such a basis, an order in
council would be unconstitutional in the English sense.
But the members of an English ministry originate and
control all important legislation in the Parliament then
sitting.   And the ministers constitute the major part,
practically the effective part, of the privy council.   And
both orders and proclamations purport to be made by
the privy council.   (Of course it is nominally the King
who makes the ordinances with the "advice" of the
council; but it is also true of acts of Parliament that
they profess to be made by the King "with the advice
and consent" of the Lords and Commons.)   Therefore the enactment of this kind of executive legislation
simply means that the ministry have demanded and received from their adherents (necessarily constituting
a majority) in Parliament permission to deal legisla-

tively either with a subject in general or with the details of a subject the outlines of which have been sketched in an act.

As stated above, those who have not studied the subject might well be surprised to learn the extent to which this power is actually employed. An English writer has recently said: "The extent to which we are governed at present by orders which hardly come within the direct cognizance of the legislature is much wider than most people are aware of." The President of Harvard, in his notable book on the British government, observes:

"Power to make ordinances which have the force of law and are binding upon the whole community is frequently given to the Crown (or more strictly to the Crown in council) by statute, notably in matters affecting public health, education, etc., and the practice is constantly becoming more and more extensive, until at present the rules made in pursuance of such powers—known as 'statutory orders'—are published every year in a volume similar in form to that containing the statutes. Some of these orders must be submitted to Parliament, but go into effect unless within a certain time an address to the contrary is passed by one of the houses, while others take effect at once, or after a fixed period, and are laid upon the tables of the houses in order to give formal notice of their adoption. In making such orders the Crown acts by virtue of a purely delegated authority, and stands in the same position as a town council. The orders are a species of subordinate legislation, and can be enacted only in strict conformity with the statutes by which the power is granted; and being delegated, not inherent in the Crown, a power of this kind does not fall within the prerogative in its narrower and more appropriate sense."[3]

[3] Lowell, "The Government of England," Vol. I, p. 20.

The passage quoted describes an interesting detail in the working of government in England, as applied to the ordinary needs and problems of government arising in times of peace. But when a country enters upon a state of war, not only are those needs and problems vastly changed, but there arises at once the necessity and the concurrent impulse to concentrate power and authority in that branch of the government which wields the sword. In such a crisis, therefore, it always happens that executive orders, decrees, and proclamations play a highly important part in the internal regulation of the country and even in its international affairs, and that there is neither time nor disposition to scrutinize closely the basis of legislative authorization on which they profess to rest.

The very words "order in council" should recall a stirring episode of American history to the minds of even American school children. For it was the British orders in council of November 11, 1807, that inaugurated England's campaign of seizing and searching neutral vessels for enemy's goods. These were countered by Napoleon's executive orders, the Berlin and Milan decrees of the same year. The result was the loss of hundreds of American ships and the almost total destruction of American commerce, which led to the embargo and non-intercourse acts, and eventually (at least as a chief contributing factor) to the war of 1812.

But nothing in the previous history of constitutional government in the world is at all comparable to what has been done by executive legislation in England since the beginning of the Great War in 1914. Limitations of space forbid us to follow this subject into all its ramifications. But it is believed that a bare outline of the principal facts cannot fail to be impressive. On the 27th of November, 1914, Parliament passed the "Defense of the Realm Consolidation Act" (5 Geo. V, c. 8). This simply provided that

"his majesty in council has power during the continuance of the present war to issue regulations for securing the public safety and the defense of the realm."

It would be difficult to imagine how more unlimited powers of law-making could be granted to the council, that is, the Prime Minister and his associates, than by this statute. It has been said:

"The provisions of this act practically place the whole country under martial law, but it is to be noted that the restrictions on the liberty of the subject and on the freedom of the expression of opinion are only to continue during the present war."

In pursuance of this act, and on the very day following its enactment, a set of "Defense of the Realm Regulations" were made and put in force by an order in council. These regulations contain sixty-three articles or sections, and make elaborate and detailed provisions for putting the country on a war basis, for requisitioning or employing its manufacturing and industrial resources, for its external defense, for preventing the giving of aid or information to the enemy, against sedition, against espionage and sabotage, making new regulations of navigation, and making violations of the regulations criminal offenses, and providing for their trial before a court martial or a court of summary jurisdiction. And subsequent regulations, made under the same authority, have carried the whole matter into much greater detail, and have brought in various new subjects, such as the important matter of food conservation. Parliament of course remained in session and continued to play its important role in the government of the country and the prosecution of the war. Though it had delegated immense authority, it did not abdicate. But under its express or tacit authority executive legislation on matters of vital interest continued. The list of articles to be deemed contraband of war and to be treated as such was set forth in an executive proclamation, as were also the provisions against trading with the enemy. And the provision for adopting and putting in force as law the so-called "Declaration of London," affecting neutral ships and trade, was made by an order in council.

Canada had a somewhat similar experience in 1917 and 1918. In consequence of the necessity of a general election, there was an intermission of six months between the dissolution of one Parliament and the assembling of the next, and during all this time the government was carried on, not only as to administration, but as to the making of all laws considered necessary in view of the conditions created by the war, entirely by the ministry, without specific parliamentary authorization, by means of orders in council. Such orders, so made, are described by a writer on the subject as "a comprehensive, flexible, speedy, and decisive instrument, particularly well adapted to the exigencies of war-time." In the Canadian use of the term an "order in council" purports to be made by the Governor General in (or by the advice of) the council. Technically it cannot become effective without his signature. But just as the acts of the British Parliament speak in the voice of the sovereign and must receive the royal assent, though the King's power of veto has not been exercised since the time of Queen Anne, so the consent and signature of the Governor General of Canada to an order in council is only formal, and cases must be rare indeed in which they would be refused. Actually such an order is a law or decree based upon, and drawn in accordance with, a decision of the cabinet and signed by the President of Council or the Prime Minister or a representative of either. The work of the council, performed in such an intermission, is of course subject to be overridden and abrogated by an act of Parliament. But so could any act of any previous Parliament be swept away. It would be a mistake, therefore, to regard these orders in council as in any sense provisional or tentative, since they do not require to be confirmed by act of Parliament, and since they could be abolished only in the same manner and by the same power required for the repeal of a statute. And it must be remembered that the ministry can remain in power only so long as they can command a majority in the House of Commons, so that it is easily conceivable that the attempt to repeal an order in council, if it affected a matter of high moment, might precipitate a cabinet crisis or even lead to a dissolution.

Without attempting an exhaustive enumeration of all the details covered by the Canadian orders in council during the period mentioned, from September, 1917, to March, 1918, to mention some of the most important steps taken will illustrate the wide range and extraordinary flexibility of this instrument of government. First, the ministry provided in this way for the working out and enforcement of the military conscription act. Then orders in council created two new departments of the government with responsible ministers at their head, the Department of Immigration and Colonization and the Department of Soldiers' Civil Re-establishment. By the same agency there came into being two important sub-committees of the cabinet, the War Committee and the Reconstruction Committee. Orders in council provided for a comprehensive program of shipbuilding, for the establishment of a bureau or committee of public information, for the creation of a war trade board, for the reform of the civil service and the abolition of patronage, for a system of general registration designed to make effective for mobilization the resources and the man power of the country, and for the superseding of the Food Controller by the Canadian Food Board of three men. These orders in council also included very stringent regulations controlling the manufacture, importation, and transportation of intoxicating liquors, and regulations governing the packing industry, which in effect limited the permissible profits of houses engaged in that business to a maximum of eleven per cent on the capital invested. In all this it is said that the government were mindful of the wishes and preferences of the people and did not lack the support of public opinion. It was an experiment to have the laws of a country, and laws of transcendent importance, made by a small group of citizens who, at the time, were not acting as legislators at all, but solely as executive officers, and during a period of time which, considering the tremendous pressure of war, might be considered as equivalent to a generation of peace. Yet the claim is made that the cause of democracy has not thereby suffered, but that, on the contrary, this radically undemocratic procedure has demonstrated the fundamentally democratic character of the Canadian system of government.

That legislation may be effected by means of executive orders or decrees, during the interval between sittings of the legislative body, is a doctrine entirely unknown in the United States, where, on the other hand, it is the practice to call a special session of Congress when legislation is needed to meet an emergency But traces of the doctrine are found in the constitutional systems of some European countries, as, for example, in Denmark, where the 25th article of the Constitution of 1866 provides that

"in cases of special urgency the King may, when the Rigsdag is not in session, issue laws of temporary application, which, however, shall not be contrary to the constitution and which shall be submitted to the Rigsdag at its next session."

The other principle—that it is within the scope of executive authority to make ordinances supplementing the statutes or providing for their effective execution —is a familiar and probably useful feature of the constitutional practice of the continental nations. As to France, for instance, a work written by the present President of the Republic states that

"in order to supervise and insure the execution of the laws, the President issues general decrees, sometimes prepared by the services affected, sometimes further elaborated by the Council of State, and always countersigned by the Ministers. These are known as by-laws of public administration. They may complete the law as to points indicated by the legislator, but they cannot modify it."[4]

Executive decrees have come to play a very important part in the government of the countries of Central and South America. The constitutions of most of those states give to their presidents the power to make such ordinances and regulations as they may deem necessary to facilitate and insure the execution of the laws, though in Venezuela this may be done only "when a law so requires or authorizes in its text." In five countries (the Argentine, Honduras, Nicaragua, Paraguay, and Venezuela) the constitutions have been very careful to limit this presidential power by providing that executive ordinances or regulations must not in any way "alter the spirit or reason of the law." In Bolivia, the President may issue

"decrees and orders necessary for the execution of the laws, but without any private (or personal) definition of rights or alteration of those defined by the law, and without contravening its dispositions."

In Haiti and Ecuador, the chief executive

"is to make all regulations and decrees necessary for the purpose of executing the laws, but without power ever to suspend or interpret the laws, acts, and decrees themselves nor to dispense with their execution."

The most detailed provision is found in the Constitution of Cuba (article 68) as follows:

"The President has power to approve and promulgate the laws, and to execute them and cause them to be executed; to prescribe when Congress shall not have done so, regulations for the better execution of the laws, and further, to issue decrees and orders which he may deem

[4] Raymond Poincaré, "How France is Governed," p. 174.

necessary to that end and so far as pertains to the government and administration of the state, but without contravening, in any case, what is established by the said laws."

A complete catalogue of executive ordinances made under these constitutional provisions would be tedious and not specially edifying. But for the purpose of showing how far and in what varied directions government by executive decree can be carried in Latin America, here follows a list selected almost at random from among the matters regulated by such decrees in those countries within a period of not more than six months. It will be observed that some of them reflect extraordinary conditions created by the war, but others have no such foundation.

In Argentina, Bolivia, and Mexico executive decrees have regulated the importation and coinage of gold and prohibited its exportation.

An executive decree in Colombia authorizes the government to contract a loan not to exceed $3,000,-000 gold.

By an executive decree in Guatemala, exemption from active military service and training is obtainable upon the payment of 100 pesos, gold, annually.

Executive order No. 117 in the Dominican Republic authorizes the establishment of a food controller to regulate the exportation of food stuffs, control the importation of the same, fix their price for sale or exchange, regulate their distribution, and

"do such other things concerning food stuffs as may be considered expedient for the public welfare."

An executive decree in Ecuador provides that the

budget of receipts and expenditures of the department of war shall be the same as that of 1917.

In Haiti, a presidential decree annuls the laws under which the government granted concessions for the construction and operation of a railway from Port au Prince to Petion-Ville.

An executive decree in Brazil authorizes the Minister of Agriculture to establish agricultural stations for the education of poor children.

In the same state a similar decree was made

"to encourage the raising of sheep and goats by co-operating with the state and municipal governments in importing sheep and goats for breeding purposes, the federal government to pay one-third of the cost."

In Chile, an executive decree authorizes the municipality of Antofagasta to contract a loan of $8,500,000, the proceeds to be used in the construction of port works in that city.

In Colombia, there was an executive decree requiring the reorganization of the national police, and providing funds for the repatriation of Colombian citizens entitled by law to return to the country; and another to regulate the teaching and practice of dentistry.

In Panama, an executive decree has been issued reducing by fifty per cent the import duties on lard.

An executive decree of Brazil empowers Brazilian insurance companies to reinsure in domestic insurance companies and in foreign insurance companies of countries not at war with Brazil.

In Costa Rica, it has been provided by executive decree that anyone desiring to leave the country must obtain a passport fifteen days beforehand.

Haiti thought it necessary to declare by executive

decree that all persons have the right to engage in the purchase and sale of all kinds of national products in the towns and cantons of the Republic.

In Panama, an executive decree forbids the importation of cattle unless accompanied by certificates viséed by consuls of Panama as to their being healthy.

An executive decree in Ecuador provides for the construction in the municipality of Guayaquil of a national macadamized highway with funds obtained from the tax on automobiles and carriages.

From Mexico we learn that

"the governor of the State of Sonora has prohibited the sale of intoxicating liquors in that state under severe penalties, and has ordered that all alcoholic beverages in the state shall be collected and destroyed."

In the United States, under the constitutional theory and practice which have prevailed up to the present time, not one of the laws (for they really are laws) mentioned above would have been enacted by any executive officer on his own initiative and authority. Each of the matters involved would have been made the subject of statutory legislation, either by Congress or by a state legislature as the case might be. But if the unhindered exercise by the executive of an ill-defined power to make laws tends in the direction of autocracy, that phrase does not measure the whole extent of the danger. For if the limitations marked out by a written constitution may with impunity be overstepped in this direction, why not in any or all? What this leads to is shown in a press despatch from Panama, dated June 22, 1918, which was carried in the principal American newspapers. It stated:

"President Urriola has issued a decree deferring for six months the elections which were set for July. The reason given for this action is that it will permit the Panama government to correct conditions in the cities of Colon and Panama and put into operation regulations requested by the American military authorities. A protest against the suspension of the elections has been made to Washington by the opposition political party, on the ground that the President's action is unconstitutional. The United States is asked to uphold the Panama constitution in accordance with the treaty."

In the United States, acts of legislation by the executive power have always hitherto found their justification in the explicit provisions either of the Constitution or of an Act of Congress. It has been remarked by an authoritative writer on the American system of government:

"The President possesses a large ordinance power—that is, authority to supplement statutes by rules and regulations covering matters of detail sometimes of very great importance. Among other things, he makes rules for the army and navy, the patent office, the customs, internal revenue, consular, and civil services. Sometimes he issues these rules in accordance with provisions of the statutes, and sometimes under his general executive power. Many of the army regulations he promulgates as commander in chief. When he makes rules for the civil service, he acts under specific provisions of the civil service law. Thus, under his power to remove, to see to the faithful execution of the laws, and to issue ordinances, the President enjoys an administrative authority of no mean dimensions."[5]

While this is undoubtedly correct, still, as to matters of general public concern, not specifically affecting a branch or department of the government service, the

[5] Charles A. Beard, "American Government and Politics'" p. 188.

rule still prevails that the President's regulations and
orders must be made in pursuance of authority previously given, if they are to have the constraining force
of law and be so recognized by the courts.

It is customary that the determinations of the executive in the field here indicated, that is, in relation
to matters of general public concern, not restricted to
the military establishment or the administrative bureaus, but of such a character that they may impinge
upon the rights or liberties of the citizens, should be
set forth in the form of presidential proclamations.
These may be conveniently divided into three classes.
First, there are proclamations intended to give notice,
information, or warning to all persons who may be
concerned, announcing some statute or treaty or some
public act or determination, or intended action of the
executive department, which otherwise might not be
so quickly or so widely promulgated. For instance, it
is usual in this manner to announce the admission of
a new state into the Union, the ratification of a treaty
with a foreign power when it contains provisions which
may affect the dealings of private persons, the intention of the United States to maintain a position of
neutrality between contending nations, or the intention
of the government to enforce the neutrality laws with
strictness. In this category also we should include
President Wilson's proclamation of December 26,
1917, announcing that he thereby took possession and
assumed control of the transportation systems of the
country.

How important this function of notification may become is shown in the case of the executive proclama-

tion of the selective draft act of 1917. The statute was assailed in the courts on the ground that it unlawfully delegated legislative powers to the President. But Judge Evans, of the Circuit Court of Appeals for the Sixth Circuit disposed of this argument in the following words:

"A careful study of the proclamation of the President now in question will show that, while the future making of regulations in the premises was foreshadowed, none were made, nor intended to be made, by or through that document. Its manifest purpose was to give the people of the United States wide, accurate, and official information of the enactment of the statutory provision now before us, and which is set out in full therein. The act required a proclamation for the purpose of giving that character of notice to all who might be subject to the draft provisions, and who were thus notified to present themselves at the proper places of registration. It was not intended that the proclamation should itself be law, but that it should give notice of the provisions of a most important statute which Congress had just enacted, and which required prompt enforcement. It is sufficient, therefore, to say that its purpose was not to add to the law, nor to make regulations, but to give to the public the most prompt and the widest possible notice of certain provisions of a new law."[6]

Generally, proclamations of this class need not be authorized or required by the Constitution or the statutes. In some cases they are issued in accordance with long-established precedents, as in the instance of neutrality proclamations. But for the most part they are the spontaneous acts of the President, and it rests in his discretion alone to determine the occasions on which they shall be issued and the subjects to which they shall relate. But it is to be noted that they add noth-

[6] Sugar vs. United States, 252 Federal Reporter, 74.

ing to the existing body of law. They notify or warn, but impose no legally enforceable command. For this reason we may also place in this group proclamations which are merely advisory or hortatory, such as those annually appointing a day of public thanksgiving.

The second class of presidential orders and proclamations will include those specifically authorized by acts of Congress. These have the force of law, but their legally compulsory effect is not derived from the will of the President but from the authority granted by Congress. They generally contain provisions for the practical execution of the statutes, or they are concerned with the filling in of details as to which the legislature has delegated its authority, or they are prompted by the occurrence of some event upon which Congress has conditioned the taking effect of a statute, or perhaps its suspension. An example may be seen in the provisions of certain of the tariff acts giving the President power to enforce or suspend the law with reference to the products of certain foreign countries, on ascertaining that reciprocal trade concessions are given or withheld, as the case may be. For another illustration we may recall the provision in the income tax acts that the returns made by taxpayers

"shall be open to inspection only upon the order of the President, under rules and regulations to be prescribed by the Secretary of the Treasury and approved by the President."

Under this authorization, a set of regulations governing the conditions under which such returns might be treated as public records and be inspected by interested persons was drawn by the Secretary, approved by the

President, and promulgated by the latter, over his signature, and under the title of an "Executive Order." Again, numerous rules and proclamations, all based on similar authorization, are made with reference to the public lands, their sale or other disposition, the opening and demarcation of forest reserves and national parks, and similar matters; to the extension or government of the classified civil service; and to a very considerable variety of other subjects which it is not necessary here to catalogue. But it may be remarked in passing that those who have not given special study to the subject have but little idea of the frequency and the bulk of these presidential proclamations or the important part they play in the actual conduct of the public business. It may be of interest to note that, for a period covering four congresses, from 1909 to 1917, the presidential proclamations occupied the respectable total of 592 of the large pages used in printing the Statutes at Large. In this division also must be included the orders and proclamations issued from the White House since the United States entered upon the Great War and relating to the effective conduct of it, though their vast importance requires their separate consideration on a later page.

The third class of executive ordinances is that which contains matter of the greatest interest for students of government and constitutional practice. It includes those which are put forth on the President's own initiative, which have the constraining force of law, and which are not based upon any direction or permission of Congress, but either upon an explicit provision of the Constitution or upon an implication drawn from its enumeration of the President's powers and duties. When, for example, he issues his call for an extra or special session of Congress, his warrant is in the provision of the Constitution that

"he may on extraordinary occasions convene both houses or either of them, and in case of disagreement between them with respect to the time of adjournment, he may adjourn them to such time as he shall think proper."

A proclamation of general pardon or amnesty (such as followed upon the decision of the Supreme Court that the courts of the United States had no power to grant a suspension of the sentence imposed upon a convicted criminal during his good behavior) is clearly referable to the President's independent and constitutional authority to "grant reprieves and pardons for offenses against the United States." It is not necessary to enlarge upon his powers as commander in chief. But after this we enter upon a debatable ground, where constitutional authority for a presidential ordinance which is entirely independent of any concurrence on the part of Congress, and which shall yet have the force of law, is not very easily discernible, unless it can be drawn from the broad but indefinite provision that the President "shall take care that the laws be faithfully executed."

President Lincoln's emancipation proclamation of January 1, 1863, was stated to be made

"by virtue of the power in me vested as commander in chief of the army and navy of the United States, in time of actual armed rebellion against the authority and government of the United States, and as a fit and necessary war measure for suppressing said rebellion."

But on the other hand, his proclamation declaring a

blockade of the southern ports (April 19, 1861) was issued after he had called a special session of Congress, and was stated to be founded on the necessity of preserving the public peace, suppressing unlawful acts of insurrection, and protecting the lives and property of law-abiding citizens "until Congress shall have assembled and deliberated on said unlawful proceedings or until the same shall have ceased." It must be remembered that this action was taken in the very early stages of the war. The inference to be drawn from the language of the proclamation is that Lincoln's consciousness was not yet fully aroused to the vast magnitude of his powers as commander in chief; that he was still looking to the legislative branch of the government either to deal decisively with the situation by laws or to clothe him definitely with authority which he was not confident of possessing; that he felt his action to be provisional, if not temporary; but that he saw clearly that the crisis demanded his vigorous intervention as chief magistrate of the nation, since a duty to "take care that the laws be faithfully executed" certainly connotes an obligation to see that they are not defied and annulled. But after three anxious and momentous years Lincoln's point of view had changed. It would almost appear that, by that time, he had come to regard his military powers as adequate not only to the ordering of all such steps as were necessary to the prosecution of the war or conducive to its successful issue, but also to the adjustment of situations not directly involved in the war, but which the war had brought about; and, as a corollary to this, that any pronouncement of Congress on such matters was but little more than advisory. For on July 8, 1864, he issued a proclamation relating to the reconstruction of the governments of the southern states, in which he put into force the main provisions of a bill which had been passed by Congress on the same subject, but to which he had applied the "pocket veto" because there were some features of it to which he could not agree.

His successor, Andrew Johnson, notwithstanding his long and stubborn fight with Congress, or perhaps because of the position in which it placed him, was meticulously careful that such action as he took on his own initiative should bear the warrant of constitutional authority at least upon its face. His proclamations opening most of the southern ports to commerce, granting general amnesty and pardons, and restoring the operation of the writ of habeas corpus were prima facie supported by the powers clearly granted to the President. But the proclamations which he issued in 1865, appointing provisional governors for the states lately in insurrection, as a part of his reconstruction program, were explicitly based on the provision of the Constitution that the United States shall guarantee to every state in the Union a republican form of government, and on the fact that the President is made by the Constitution the commander in chief

"as well as chief civil executive officer of the United States, and is bound by solemn oath faithfully to execute the office of President of the United States, and to take care that the laws be faithfully executed."

President Roosevelt, as has been earlier stated, had a conviction that the constitutional provision that "the executive power shall be vested in a President of the

United States of America" vested an undefined residuum of power in the chief magistrate, limited, it is true, by the Constitution and the laws of Congress in certain particulars, but, where not so limited, to be exercised by him in his discretion as a sort of general trustee for the welfare of the public. Naturally, therefore, he found presidential proclamations and executive orders a convenient means of carrying out some of his policies without asking Congress for specific authority. Thus, he tells us:

"In a number of instances the legality of executive acts of my administration was brought before the courts. They were uniformly sustained. For example, prior to 1907, statutes relating to the disposition of coal lands had been construed as fixing the flat price at $10 to $20 per acre. The result was that valuable coal lands were sold for wholly inadequate prices, chiefly to big corporations. By executive order the coal lands were withdrawn and not opened for entry until proper classification was placed thereon by government agents. There was a great clamor that I was usurping legislative power; but the acts were not assailed in court until we brought suits to set aside entries made by persons and associations to obtain larger areas than the statutes authorized. This position was opposed on the ground that the restrictions imposed were illegal; that the executive orders were illegal. The Supreme Court sustained the government."[7]

Since the fateful sixth of April, 1917, executive orders, proclamations, and regulations have played a part in the government of our people and in the conduct of their daily lives absolutely without a parallel in our previous history. They have closely and intimately touched the lives, the liberty, the property, the food, clothing, comfort, habits, and business of all the

[7] Theodore Roosevelt, "Autobiography," p. 376.

citizens of the United States, to say nothing of the
millions of aliens within our gates. Such is the inevitable necessity of war. The phenomenon is one to
be accepted ungrudgingly by the loyal citizen. To the
student of government it presents a problem in constitutional law and practice. These orders and regulations have been issued either directly by the President or by subordinate officers to whom he has delegated the necessary authority in the premises. In
each instance, the form and substance of the rules (if
not always the manner of their execution) have been
rested upon the firm foundation of the law of the land,
as distinguished from anything like the mere will or
command of the executive. That is, the President's
orders and proclamations have been distinctly authorized either by the Constitution itself, by acts of Congress previously existing, or by new laws made to meet
the occasion. But having said this much, one cannot
fail further to remark upon the radical difference between the manner in which the authority was granted
in the United States and the method pursued in England. There, as already pointed out, the "Defense of
the Realm Consolidation Act" (1914) granted to the
council (or cabinet) practically unlimited power "to
issue regulations for securing the public safety and the
defense of the realm"; and this was done in one brief
sentence, without specification of details, and without
limitation of time except as found in the words "during the continuance of the present war." It was a
placing of the entire authority of Parliament in commission, a blanket mortgage upon the government of
the country. In the United States, on the other hand,

the situation has been dealt with in a manner which is perhaps illustrative of the entire difference between the "cabinet" or "ministerial" system of government and the "presidential" system. For in America each separate or successive exigency growing out of the war or involved in its prosecution has been made the subject of a separate act of Congress. It is true that some of these statutes have granted exceedingly broad powers to the President, and some have left an infinity of details to his unqualified discretion. But in each instance it is the formal enactment of the legislative body from which those powers are derived and by which the exercise of that discretion is justified. It is true also that most of the program of war measures was dictated by the President, in the sense that Congress looked to him for guidance and stood ready to grant, and did successively grant, whatever powers he asked for, upon his representing the necessity either by message or in a personal address. But instead of the President demanding, or Congress conceding at one stroke, an unbounded power to govern the country and make its laws by executive decree during the war, it was the understanding and practice of both branches of the government that the regulatory power of the chief magistrate should be defined and advanced step by step, so that there might be specific warrant of law for his dealing with each separate subject.

This was so from the initial scene. It is the constitutional prerogative of Congress to declare war, and of the President to conduct it. It was from Congress therefore that the declaration proceeded of a state of war between the United States and Germany, April 6,

1917, and between the United States and Austria, December 7, 1917. And in each case the joint resolution declaring war contained a provision that

"the President be, and he is hereby, authorized and directed to employ the entire naval and military forces of the United States and the resources of the government to carry on war against"

the enemy. But it is precisely at this point that the divergence began between the English method of granting war powers to the executive and that followed in the United States. For the resolution, as it was originally proposed in the Senate, authorized and directed the President

"to take immediate steps not only to put the country into a thorough state of defense, but also to exert all its power and employ all of its resources to carry on war against the Imperial German Government and to bring the conflict to a successful termination."

But the committee to which the resolution was referred evidently felt that the concession of a power so limitless and complete, a power to wield all the power and command all the resources of the nation, meant nothing less than the virtual abdication of the Congress and its effective exclusion from all co-operation in determining upon the necessity and expedience of such measures as might be proposed. The committee struck out the words quoted and substituted an authorization and direction to the President to "employ the entire naval and military forces of the United States and the resources of the government" to carry on the war. The change of language is most significant. The committee's amendment does not appear to have been debated in the Senate. The resolution was passed as reported, and was sent in that form to the House and there concurred in.

The President's first war proclamation, issued on the very day of the declaration of war, related to the conduct of alien enemies found within the United States and the various restraints necessary to be imposed upon their freedom of action and the places where they might reside. This proclamation established regulations which were absolutely compulsory and which would be backed, wherever necessary, by the entire force of the country. Here undoubtedly the President made laws; but he acted under an explicit delegation of authority. For an act of Congress dating back to 1798, and now contained in sections 4067 to 4070 of the Revised Statutes, provides that when the United States is at war and the President makes public proclamation of the fact, he is authorized

"by his proclamation or other public act, to direct the conduct to be observed on the part of the United States towards the aliens who become so liable, the manner and degree of the restraint to which they shall be subject, and in what cases, and upon what security their residence shall be permitted, and to provide for the removal of those who, not being permitted to reside within the United States, refuse or neglect to depart therefrom, and to establish any other regulations which are found necessary in the premises and for the public safety."

And the President's alien-enemy proclamation expressly stated that he acted "under and by virtue of the authority vested in me by the Constitution of the United States and the said sections of the Revised Statutes."

It will be unnecessary to scrutinize each of the important presidential proclamations bearing on the war. But a survey of the chief acts of Congress having to do with the matter will disclose a steady and determined purpose to grant to the executive every needful or expedient power, but to grant each successive instalment of authority in unmistakable terms, so that there might never be doubt of the legal sanction of the President's decrees or regulations. The orders for the seizing of ships in American ports owned by Germans were based upon a joint resolution of Congress

"authorizing the President to take over for the United States the possession and title of any vessel within its jurisdiction, which at the time of coming therein was owned in whole or in part by any corporation, citizen, or subject of any nation with which the United States may be at war."

The selective draft act was entitled "An act to authorize the President to increase temporarily the military establishment of the United States," and it provided, among other things, that "the President be, and he is hereby, authorized . . . to draft into the military service of the United States" the members of the National Guard, and "to raise by draft as herein provided, organize, and equip an additional force of 500,-000 enlisted men, or such part or parts thereof as he may at any time deem necessary"; and "the President is further authorized, in his discretion and at such time as he may determine, to raise and begin the training of an additional force of 500,000 men." The espionage act contains a typical grant of authority to be exercised upon the judgment and in the discretion of the executive. It provides:

"Whenever during the present war the President shall

find that the public safety shall so require, and shall make proclamation thereof, it shall be unlawful to export from or ship from or take out of the United States to any country named in such proclamation any article or articles mentioned in such proclamation, except at such time or times, and under such regulations and orders, and subject to such limitations and exceptions, as the President shall prescribe, until otherwise ordered by the President or by Congress."

The same purpose and the same method are apparent in the statute which has perhaps more nearly touched the daily lives of the people than any other, entitled "An act to provide further for the national security and defense by encouraging the production, conserving the supply, and controlling the distribution of food products and fuel." This act, approved August 10, 1917, provides that "the President is authorized to make such regulations and to issue such orders as are essential effectively to carry out the provisions of this act." And the President's proclamation setting in motion the vast machinery of the food and fuel administrations (August 14, 1917) was explicitly based upon this grant of authority. So it was also with the statute to regulate and punish trading with the enemy and providing a custodian of alien enemy property; and with the act of May 16, 1918, "to authorize the President to provide housing for war needs"; and with the so-called "Overman act," entitled "An act authorizing the President to co-ordinate or consolidate executive bureaus, agencies, and offices, in the interest of economy and the more efficient concentration of the government."

Finally, attention should be given to the very important proclamation of the President taking over the railway systems of the country, because it is evident that it was drawn with very great care, and because it is very explicit as to the source of his authority. This proclamation, dated December 26, 1917, begins with a recital of the declaration of war as having been made by "the Congress of the United States in the exercise of the constitutional authority vested in them." Next it repeats the provision of an act of August 29, 1916, to the effect that

"the President in time of war is empowered, through the Secretary of War, to take possession and assume control of any system or systems of transportation, or any part thereof, and to utilize the same, to the exclusion so far as may be necessary of all other traffic thereon, for the transfer or transportation of troops, war material and equipment, or for such other purposes connected with the emergency as may be needful or desirable."

The proclamation continues:

"And whereas it has now become necessary in the national defense to take possession and assume control of certain systems of transportation and to utilize the same, to the exclusion so far as may be necessary of other than war traffic thereon, for the transportation of troops, war material and equipment therefor, and for other needful and desirable purposes connected with the prosecution of the war; Now therefore I, Woodrow Wilson, President of the United States, under and by virtue of the powers vested in me by the foregoing resolutions and statute, and by virtue of all other powers thereto me enabling, do hereby, through Newton D. Baker, Secretary of War, take possession and assume control at twelve o'clock noon on the 28th day of December, 1917, of each and every system of transportation, and the appurtenances thereof, located wholly or in part within the boundaries of the continental United States, and consisting of railroads," etc.

Nevertheless a United States District Court, having

to consider the effect of this proclamation in a suit before it, to which one of the commandeered roads was a party,[8] has said:

"The proposition is so well established as to be elementary that Congress may authorize heads of departments or other officers to make regulations within certain limits, and, when made within those limits, such regulations have the force and effect of law, and may be enforced as such; but it has often been held that the delegation of authority to make regulatory orders gives no power to add to, take from, or modify the limitations prescribed by Congress."

Now the act of August 29, 1916, authorizing the President to take possession of the railroads through the Secretary of War,

"does not give authority to the President to make or promulgate a proclamation of any character. No one, however, could or would contend that he had not abundant authority to issue such documents whenever he thought it proper to give notice or information to the public. But such papers cannot have any effect as laws, in the absence of express constitutional or congressional authorization."

Consequently the court felt constrained to hold that the proclamation in question, in so far as it appointed the Secretary of the Treasury to be "director general of railroads" and provided other details in regard to the control and operation of the roads, *has no force as law,* that is, it cannot affect or modify the legal rights or obligations of any person or corporation.

---

[8] Muir vs. Louisville & Nashville Railroad Company, 247 Federal Reporter, 888.

VII

EXECUTIVE POWER IN THE STATES

The governments of the states were moulded into
their first form upon the same theory of the relations
between the executive and the legislature as that which
came to prevail in the formation of the federal Constitution and the early operation of the government
under it. Indeed, the general acceptance of this theory
among the men of leading and influence in the states
may be said to have predetermined its destiny as a
guiding principle in the working of the national government. The constitutions adopted in the Revolutionary period recognized the importance of separating
the three main departments of government and made
suitable provision to that end, and none more clearly
and explicitly than that of Massachusetts, in 1780.
But the purpose, declared with equal explicitness, was
"that this may be a government of laws and not of
men." That was the idea which lay back of all the
precautions taken by the early constitution makers—
the fear of the tyrannical exercise of power by individual men in office. Very close to them were the
memories of the almost unlimited powers vested in
some of the colonial governors and their arbitrary and
high-handed exercise. Nor was it easy to exorcise the
bogie of that stubborn and meddling monarch George
III. It is no wonder that the men of that day should

have had a profound distrust of executive power and serious apprehensions as to the possibility of its abuse. To their minds it was clear that a chief executive officer was needed, and that the discharge of purely administrative functions by the legislative body was neither suitable nor safe. Yet their conception of the legislature as the supreme power in the state, and as the possessor of such "sovereignty" as might be conceded to exist among a free people, was equally fixed. Hence it followed that the law-making department was to be predominant. The governor was to be strictly confined to the somewhat narrow prerogatives which were somewhat grudgingly granted to him. He was not to be the ruler, the leader, or the dictator of policies or of laws. It will not be forgotten that several of the early state constitutions even provided for the choosing of the governor by the legislature.

So much for theory. But the actual evolution of the state governments has shown an endeavor on the part of the executive office to extricate itself from some of the restraints placed upon it, and a tendency on the part of the people to retrieve from the field of legislative exercise some of the functions and duties which are properly executive in their nature and to bestow them where they rightfully belong. Perhaps this does not indicate a changing belief as to the relative importance of the executive and legislative departments, nor any deliberate purpose to shift the leadership from the one to the other. Rather it resulted from a gradual but accelerating conviction in the minds of the people that the functioning of their state legislatures was becoming—had indeed become—grossly unsatisfactory and disappointing. From the middle of **the** nineteenth century there became apparent a remarkably wide-spread distrust of the legislatures. Their powers had been abused; they had failed to register the real desires of the people; often they had thwarted the popular will; some of their enactments were impracticable, others downright foolish; they were not free from the taint of corruption; legislators were purchasable; it was only too conspicuously evident that at times they were unworthily dominated by unscrupulous business interests. Hence there came an era chiefly distinguished for the successive application of curbs upon the powers of the legislatures. From time to time, as the people had opportunity to amend or revise their constitutions, they sought to delimit more sharply the permissible activity of the legislative body. But practically all these reforms were negative rather than positive in character. That is, the effort was not so much to improve legislative doings or promote the making of good laws as to minimize the legislature's power for harm.

Thus there began to appear in the constitutions provisions relating to legislative procedure, as, that each bill shall relate to but one single subject, which shall be plainly expressed in the title, and that laws shall not be amended nor their provisions extended by mere reference, but that such modifications or extensions must be effected by re-enactment at length. The general prohibitions against local and special legislation having proved ineffectual, the constitutions began to be encumbered with a long list of subjects, generally of this character, as to which the legislature is forbid-

den to act at all. The sessions of the legislative body
were made shorter and less frequent. That is, biennial sessions were generally substituted for annual assemblies, and the number of days during which the
session might continue was cut down to narrow limits.
This drew forth from one observer the remark that

"for a people claiming pre-eminence in the sphere of
popular government, it seems hardly creditable that in
their seeming despair of a cure for the chronic evils of
legislation, they should be able to mitigate them only by
making them intermittent."

Again the practice began and has continued of in-
corporating into every new constitution a host of provisions which are purely of a statutory nature and
therefore have no fitting place in the fundamental law.
This practice of overloading the constitutions has
worked infinite harm, since it has tended to confuse the
real distinction between true and essential principles
of government and merely ephemeral pieces of legislation, and has distinctly lowered the respect of the people for their organic laws. But it seemed the only way
in which certain subjects of high importance could be
removed from the grasp of the legislature; and the
utter lack of public confidence in such bodies could not
be more strikingly manifested than in the adoption of
this otherwise indefensible method of securing a certain measure of continuity and immunity from meddling for laws considered to be of especial importance
in the policy of the state. Finally, the popular initiative and the compulsory referendum in legislation are
advocated by their friends almost entirely on the
ground that they give the people an additional means

of control over an unresponsive, extravagant, faithless, or corrupt legislature.

In the federal government we have seen the theory of the supremacy of the legislative branch gradually give way to the leadership of the executive. Whatever else may be said of this change, it cannot be denied that it has resulted in the development of a strong, efficient, and well co-ordinated government. But the process in the states has been very different. The curtailment of the powers of the legislatures and the withdrawal from them of the respect and confidence of the people have not been compensated by any corresponding enlargement of the powers and influence of the governors. Rather, the period of which we are speaking has been described as one of "decentralization and disintegration of the executive." And the consequence is that the state governments today constitute the weak link in our chain of political institutions.

Since approximately the time of the Civil War, the legislative output of the states has taken on a different complexion and their administrative business has enormously increased. This has been due to the introduction into daily life of the splendid acquisitions of science, to the steadily increasing complexity of social and industrial conditions, and to the rise of that new democracy which grounds its teachings upon human brotherhood and finds its best expression in the voice of an awakened public conscience. In the interests of the public welfare and for the protection of the individual, no less than for the encouragement of enterprise and the enrichment of the life of the community through an increase of the prosperity of the whole, the states have had to turn their attention, in both their legislative and administrative departments, to the railroads, telegraphs, and telephone systems, and the various other public utilities which have become indispensable ministrants to the public convenience and comfort; to the systematic enlargement and improvement of the methods and means of public education; to the regulation of banking and the business of insurance; to the conservation and beneficial use of natural resources and the encouragement of agriculture; to modern theories and practices in the matter of public sanitation; to new and vital ideas in the domain of organized charities and of preventive and correctional police; to the reform and reorganization of the municipal governments; and to the regulation of industry and commerce, for the prevention of injustice and oppression and for ameliorating the lot of the vast army of workers.

All this work required a substructure of legislation. But after legislation comes administration. General rules, principles, and policies having been laid down in the laws, the working out of their details and their application in actual practice to an infinite complexity of cases is the task of the administrative department. But (speaking necessarily in the most general terms) the entry of the state into these new fields of regulation and control has not tended either to strengthen the influence of the governor or materially to increase the sphere of his official activity. Almost universally the disposition has been to commit the administration of all these various new departments to new executive officers, popularly elected, and therefore owing no de-

ference or allegiance to the governor of the state other
than such as may spring from considerations of party
interest, or else to boards and commissions specially
created for the purpose, and whose members, if in the
first instance they owe their appointment to the governor, are not invariably subject to his power of removal, and are only in a slight degree responsible to
him or subject to his control. In several of the states,
there are now more than one hundred such separate
executive officers, boards, commissions, or other administrative agencies. It has not inaptly been termed
an age of "government by commissions." The result
is that the governor of a state is not vested with the
power of control and the corresponding responsibility
which clearly belong to the head of the executive department. He is the chief magistrate only in name
and appearance. To a very limited extent he is an executive officer; to an infinitely greater extent he is only
a political officer.

The contrast between the growth of executive power
in the federal government and its decline in the state
governments has been well stated in the following
passage:

"Originally occupying about the same relative position
[as the President] the governor has been stripped of his
administrative power and confined to the exercise of political powers, while the President has been gaining more
and more administrative power, until at the present time
he makes or unmakes the administration of the United
States. It has become impossible for the governor to
become the head of the commonwealth administration
because the people have decided that he shall be in the
main a political officer. They have lessened his power
of appointment. They have almost destroyed his power

of removal. He has been unable to develop any power of direction. The governor's office has been deprived of all means of administrative development."[1]

Still it is an undeniable fact that the people of the average state do look to the governor as their leader. They feel that he is the one person who most truly represents the embodied power and dignity of the state and the collective will of its people. However unjustly, he is the one who is held responsible for the government of the state during his administration. It may be that there survives some ancient veneration for the office of the governor, some inarticulate memory of great men who guided the destinies of the state in past days. It may be because the governorship is the chief political prize within the state. It is perhaps more likely because such powers and prerogatives as still remain to the governor are his exclusively, to be shared with no one else, so that the light which plays upon his official doings is focussed upon the individual, instead of being refracted from the many facets of a composite executive. But whatever the cause, the fact remains that the governor is still the most conspicuous figure in the state administration, and if his powers were sufficiently strengthened, and supposing him to possess an adequate natural endowment and experience, the one best fitted both to represent and to lead the people. To an appreciable extent, a state governor is forced into that very position. It is his constitutional duty to address the legislature (in person or by message) upon the activities, the policies,

[1] Goodnow, "Comparative Administrative Law," p. 81, as quoted in Finley's "The American Executive," p. 46.

and the needs of the state, and to recommend the enactment of such laws as he deems salutary or expedient. Thereby he assumes a distinct responsibility
towards the public, but it is a responsibility which is
unjustly laid upon his shoulders if he is unable to
carry his plans into effect. His may be a "voice crying
in the wilderness," but he is blamed if the hosts do
not assemble in answer to his call.

Signs are not wanting, however, of a popular disposition to confide more to the governor, while exact-
ing more from him. A publicist of distinction, recently the governor of his state, has said:

"The people look to the governor, and not to the individual members of the legislature, for leadership and
for the passage of such laws as the economic, political,
and social condition of the state may demand, and judge
his administration by his success or failure in securing
the enactment of necessary laws. There is profound distrust by the people of the United States of their legislatures and serious suspicion as to the source of legislation, and this distrust and suspicion are intensified by the
dark-lantern methods which prevail, and the secret, invisible government by which these bodies are so often
dominated. The people of the United States want their
governors to be leaders in legislation, for they alone represent the entire state, and they favor such constitutional
revision as will make their leadership secure and effective."[2]

It is true that some of the state governors, like
Theodore Roosevelt in New York, have assumed and
exercised the functions of leadership with notable energy and often with no less remarkable results. But
this has been due to the dynamic character of the man

[2] Hon. Emmet O'Neal in Virginia Law Register, December,
1917, p. 166.

himself, rather than to any peculiarity in the constitutions of those states. Such governors have simply laid hold upon the possibilities of the situation. But their conduct has been exceptional, not typical. As explaining how an executive of such force of character may make his personality felt, rather than as delineating any common or general process of executive leadership in government, attention may well be given to the following passage from an important study of the state governments, quite recently published:

"Since the governor is armed with the appointing and veto powers, his recommendations are bound to be considered regardless of his party affiliation. If he is disposed to make a vigorous use of these powers in order to promote a legislative program of his own, he becomes a more influential legislator than any single member of the legislature itself, not even excepting the speaker. Public recognition of this fact has caused the governor to accept a responsibility which the framers of the original state constitutions would have regarded as unconstitutional, for the action of the legislature upon the principal public issues. Executive usurpation of legislative prerogatives has been sanctioned by public opinion, because the governor has tended to stand for the interests of the state as a whole, being elected in the state at large, whilst the members of the legislature have only too often stood for local and private interests within their several districts."[3]

There seems to be a general conviction that the time has come to rescue the state governments from this unsatisfactory condition and to make them as strong and efficient in their proper sphere as the federal government has become. But apparently the people despair of reforming their legislatures. Proposals in that be-

[3] Arthur N. Holcombe, "State Government in the United States," p. 268.

half are almost invariably confined to the idea that
the output of laws might be improved if the number
of members of the legislature were greatly reduced,
and perhaps that the legislative body should be reor-
ganized as a single small chamber. On the other hand,
public opinion has strongly turned to the executive department as the field in which beneficial change may
most readily be brought about, with a helpful reaction
upon the entire system of state administration. To
enlarge the powers of the governor, to strengthen his
influence, to invest him with the right to initiate, direct,
and control legislation and with authority over practically all the other state officers, and so to place him
frankly in a position where he may assume the leadership of the state, charging him with a corresponding
responsibility—this is the plan of reform most widely
and vigorously advocated. The discussion of the subject must first of all recognize the fact that the problem of the relation between the executive and legislative departments is not at all the same in the states as it
is in the United States. It grows out of a different set
of conditions, and it is by no means certain that it
could or should be solved in the same way. The governmental machinery of a state is different from that
of the national government. Besides, presidential as-
pirations to leadership and control have not been
avowedly based on any charge that Congress had become incompetent or corrupt, while, in the states, it is
the decadence of the legislatures which is chiefly responsible for the hope that in the ascendancy of the
governor may be found the way of salvation.

First, the proposal to give the governor a direct

right of initiative in legislation grows naturally out of his constitutional authority and duty to recommend the enactment of laws upon such subjects as he deems important. The annual and other messages of the state governors do, it is true, receive considerable attention, and it may be supposed that they exercise a limited influence upon the course of legislation. But it is not invariably the case that bills are introduced in accordance with their suggestions or debate excited, and at the best the message can only outline a general policy without attempting to mould details. The governor's duty to recommend legislation may plausibly be said to imply a further duty to use every proper means to see that his recommendations bear fruit. But no such means are constitutionally at his command. He can only resort to personal urgency or political pressure. It is no matter of surprise, then, that measures which the governor himself considers of the utmost importance, or which he is most strongly pledged to advocate, sometimes receive but lukewarm consideration at the hands of the legislature, and if they are not secretly done to death by sinister influences, are committed to unbroken repose in the files of the committee room.

The remedy proposed is to give the governor power to suggest amendments to any bills which are presented to him for his signature, and also the right to introduce his own drafts of bills directly into either house of the legislature, and there to explain them and argue for their passage either in person or through the heads of executive departments. What might be expected from such a change of methods has been thus expounded by

a writer whose own experience as the governor of his
state entitles him to speak with authority:

"With the power of amendment, which should not be
overcome except by a two-thirds vote, with authority to
submit his recommendations either in person or by written message, and to present these recommendations in the
form of bills, and to defend them on the floor of the
legislature in open debate, such bills to enjoy precedence
on the calendar of both houses over all other bills except
appropriations, the governor would assume that position
of leadership which would guarantee efficient and vigorous administration. If bad laws are passed, the governor is generally held responsible at the bar of public
opinion, and hence he should be armed with power to
make his leadership effective, as the responsible chief of
state. This increase of the power of the executive would
tend to better and more responsible legislation and make
the governor directly responsible for the laws enacted
during his administration."[4]

It has even been suggested that the best results might
be obtained by giving to the executive department a
constitutional monopoly of the initiative in legislation.
Certainly this goes too far. At the same time it is an
incontrovertible fact that the business of a legislative
session is directed and controlled either by a leader or
band of leaders within the house, by a political boss
or bosses, by organized outside influences, or by a
combination among some or all of these sources of
power. Nothing is accomplished except by personal
initiative and personal influence. The mass of legislators must either be pushed or led.

"It is a cardinal fact, to be recognized in the construction of legislative bodies, that the ultimate and all-im-
portant duty and function of the people, and even of

[4] Hon. Emmet O'Neal, in the Virginia Law Register, December, 1917, p. 166.

their representative bodies, must be simply to assent and
dissent. To a single leader or group of leaders must fall
the responsibility of initiative, of interpreting, crystalliz-
ng, and formulating the vague and dormant thoughts of
the people, and submitting their formulations to them for
correction and adjustment. We must set up in our legislative bodies the definite machinery of initiative and assent. If we fail to do so, the actual management of legislation will continue to lie outside the control of the people, in the hands of unofficial and irresponsible leaders.
For leaders there must be."[5]

Even without giving the executive a monopoly of
the initiative, there is ground to believe that the quality of the legislative output would be greatly improved
if the governor and his chief aides could frame and introduce their own bills. Such measures could not fail
to carry a special prestige, and it is altogether probable
that they would be subjected to more careful scrutiny
and more earnest debate, and, what is most important,
both their advocates and their opponents would be
forced to come out into the light of day. It is beyond
question that one of the results would be a much
greater measure of precision, definiteness, and accuracy both in the processes of legislation and in the language of the statutes. If anyone is insensible to the
need of improvement in these respects, let him ponder
the following pieces of evidence. Governor Hodges
of Kansas is reported to have stated that, during his
incumbency of that office, although his executive clerk
and the attorney general did their best to scrutinize
all the bills before the legislature, two instances were
found in which identically the same law had been en-

[5] H. S. Gilbertson, in the National Municipal Review, November, 1917, p. 669.

acted twice in the same session, a case in which an act
had been repealed three times, a statute which was
amended by a new statute within a very few days after
its enactment, and a law, passed in 1911, which was
repealed in 1913, and then, after being· so repealed,
was at the same session amended and again repealed.
And in the same line a recent writer observes that
while, with respect to other classes of legislative work,

"the failure of the legislatures is to a certain extent a
matter of opinion, with respect to the drafting of legislation their incompetence is plainly recorded in the statute
books. Crude, almost illiterate, legislation is constantly
coming to light through the proceedings of the state
courts; laws which cannot be intended to mean what they
say, and laws which mean nothing, are not uncommon.
A regulation found in the road law of one state that no
one shall operate a political steam roller or band wagon
on the highway doubtless was put there in jest, but there
is nothing funny about a provision, found in the same
state, that proprietors of hotels shall keep the walls and
floors of their rooms covered with plaster. In Massachusetts, where things are supposed to be done better,
one legislature, in trying to prevent the display of the red
flag of anarchy upon the highway, succeeded in forbid-
ding Harvard students from carrying their college ban-
ner to the football field."[6]

These general ideas as to strengthening the executive
branch of the state governments have not failed to find
expression in more or less definitely formulated programs, some of which are sufficiently novel, or sufficiently radical, to require mention. For example, according to a plan proposed by Mr. Richard S. Childs,[7]

"the governor and council would prepare and introduce
budget and other legislation and get the consent of the

[6] Holcombe, "State Government in the United States," p. 270.
[7] In the National Municipal Review, November, 1917, p. 661.

lower house if they can. The lower house has the power of reducing items in the budget, and may repeal laws or enact them by passing them two years in succession in spite of the dissent of the governor and council. The governor and council having ample administrative service would originate the big legislative projects and argue for them in the lower house as administration measures. Such bills would be properly related to old law and old departments, as distinguished from individual freak bills originating with the more amateur representatives. The lower house would become a consenting body, reviewing and accepting or rejecting the projects of the more expert governor and council." Again, we are told that "a very noteworthy scheme was presented in 1918 to the legislature of Illinois, but failed to become a law. The bill provided for a joint legislative commission, composed of the governor, lieutenant governor, speaker of the house, chairmen of the committees on appropriations of the senate and the house, chairmen of the committees on judiciary of the senate and the house, together with five other senators and five other members of the house. The purpose of this commission would have been to prepare in advance of a legislative session a program of legislation, with drafts of bills on subjects investigated by the commission, and the commission was given power to that end to appoint special committees of its own members or others to study particular problems and draft bills. Nothing short of actual experience could determine the value of such a plan or the alterations that might be required in it, but it will be noted that it forces nothing on the legislature and creates no new constitutional problems."[8]

Altogether the most comprehensive, consistent, and advanced plan for the reorganization of a state's executive department was that presented to the Massachusetts Constitutional Convention, in session in the summer of 1917. This plan was drawn by Mr. Josiah Quincy of Boston, formerly the mayor of that city,

[8] Freund, "Standards of American Legislation," p. 299.

and was recommended to the favorable consideration of the convention by the unanimous vote of the committee on the executive, to which it had been referred. The program is of such importance and general interest that the resolutions in which it was embodied are here set forth in full.

"Resolved, that it is expedient to amend the Constitution by the adoption of the subjoined articles of amendment:

"1. The executive department of the government of the Commonwealth shall include all executive and administrative functions and offices and all offices not coming under the judicial or the legislative department. All state officers whose election by the people is provided for by the Constitution, shall be under the authority and control of the governor, and all such officers and employees without exception shall furnish him with any official report, information, or opinion which he may require.[9]

"2. The governor may remove any officer subject to appointment by him and coming under the executive department for such specific cause as he may assign in writing, provided that he shall first give such officer an opportunity, with three days' notice, to be heard by him upon the question of such removal and to file any reasons against the same; the order of removal and any such reasons against the same shall be filed with the secretary of the Commonwealth and shall be a public record.[10]

[9] The accompanying report of the committee on the executive explains this provision as follows: "The first amendment defines in two sentences the scope of the governor's executive authority. It subordinates to him, as supreme executive magistrate, the administrative and executive organization of the state, so far as this is, or may be, created by statute."

[10] The committee's report says that "the second amendment gives to the governor independent power of removal; this seems to the committee essential if any real responsibility is to be introduced into our administrative system."

"3. The term of office of the governor and of the lieutenant governor elected at the regular state election in the year 1918, and in every alternate year thereafter, shall be for two years from the first day of January next ensuing.[11]

"4. At the beginning of each regular session, and at such other times as he may deem proper, the governor shall give to the General Court[12] information as to the state of the Commonwealth and recommend to its consideration such measures as he shall judge necessary or expedient. He may make such recommendations either orally or by written message, to either branch of the General Court or to both branches convened in joint session; so far as practicable, he shall accompany any specific recommendations so made with drafts of bills proposed by him. Every such bill shall be designated as an executive bill and shall be before the General Court for its action, subject to any amendment thereof which the governor may make by message while the same is pending. If any such bill is referred to a committee of the General Court or of either branch thereof, a report shall be made thereon within thirty days of the date upon which the same was recommended by the governor; and after the expiration of five days from the time when it is made, such report shall be given precedence in consideration in both branches over all other reports or bills. No such executive bill shall be rejected in either branch of the General Court except by a vote taken by yeas and nays.[13]

[11] "The third amendment," says the committee, "provides for the election of the governor and lieutenant governor for a two-year term. Independent of any action which may be taken upon the general question of biennial elections, this committee believes that the chief executive at least should be given a two-year term. It seems unnecessary and undesirable to continue the practice of electing the governor annually in this Commonwealth, and it certainly hampers him seriously in the development of his policies and in giving the thought and energy which should be called for in performing the duties of his office."

[12] This is the designation given to the legislature by the Constitution of Massachusetts.

[13] The fourth amendment, the committee explains, "gives for-

"5. In case an executive bill which the governor has by message recommended to the General Court is not enacted, in a form approved and signed by him, during the session at which it was so recommended, the governor may refer such bill to the people by filing with the secretary of the Commonwealth not later than the first day of August next following a notice of such reference accompanied by a copy of the bill so recommended. The question of approving or rejecting such bill shall be placed upon the official ballot, in a form approved by the governor, and voted on at the state election, whether regular or special, next ensuing; and if such bill is approved by a majority of the voters voting thereon the same shall become law and shall take effect at the expiration of thirty days after the election at which it was approved, or at such time after the expiration of the said thirty days as may be fixed in such bill. In case any bill disapproved by the governor shall be passed by the General Court notwithstanding his objections, the same shall not take effect until thirty days from the date of such passage, and the governor shall have the right at any time within such period to suspend the operation of such bill until the same has been referred to the people by filing with the secretary of the Commonwealth a written notice of such suspension and reference. The question of approving or rejecting such bill shall be placed upon the official ballot, in a form approved by the governor, and voted on at the state election next ensuing; and if such bill is approved by a majority of the voters voting thereon the same shall become law and shall take effect at the expiration of thirty days after the election at which it was approved, or at such time after the expiration of the said thirty days as may be fixed in such bill. If any bill disapproved by the governor fails of passage by the General Court in the manner provided in the Constitution, the General Court may, by resolve which shall take effect without being laid before the governor for his ap-

mal recognition and authority, now lacking in our Constitution, to the practice established in this state no less than in others, where it has formal sanction, of executive recommendations to the legislature."

proval, refer such bill to the people in the manner and with the effect prescribed and set forth in the forty-second article of amendment of the Constitution.[14]

"6. The governor may at any time attend a session of either branch of the General Court and speak upon any pending bill. Upon the written request of the governor, any executive or administrative officer shall be admitted temporarily to a seat in either branch of the General Court with the right to speak upon any matter coming within or under his official authority, but without a right to vote; and upon the request of either branch, made through the governor, any such officer shall appear in person before it. Either branch of the General Court shall have the right to call upon the governor, or through the governor to call upon any executive or administrative officer, to furnish in writing information as to any matter coming within or under his official authority, provided that such information need not be furnished if the governor deems it incompatible with the public interest to communicate the same.[15]

[14] This highly important provision, it will be observed, gives to the governor a right to call a popular referendum on (that is, submit directly to the vote of the electorate) any bill which the legislature refuses to pass on his recommendation, and also any bill which the legislature persists in passing over his veto. The explanatory report of the committee states that: "The fifth amendment gives the governor the right to submit directly to the people, for adoption or rejection by them any executive bill which the legislature refuses to pass. It is believed by the committee that such a provision is a safe one, as the official responsibility of the governor will cause him to use such power with discretion and only when he believes that the public interest requires direct action by the people."

[15] According to the report of the committee, "the amendment numbered six is intended to bring about closer contact between the executive and legislative departments, and to bring them into better working relations with each other. As every bill passed by the legislature has to come before the governor for his action, there seems no reason why he should not take part in the discussion of any pending measure if he sees fit to do so."

"7. The governor shall have the right to return any bill within five days after it shall have been laid before him to the branch of the General Court in which it originated, with a recommendation that any amendment or amendments specified by him be made therein; such bill shall thereupon be before the General Court and subject to amendment and re-enactment, but no amendment so recommended by the governor shall be rejected in either branch except by vote taken by yeas and nays. If such bill is re-enacted in any form, it shall again be laid before the governor for his action, but he shall have no right to return the same a second time with a recommendation to amend. The governor shall have the right, before acting on any such re-enacted bill, to disapprove and strike out in the same any portion thereof which he may deem properly separable from the remainder, provided that within five days of the time when such bill was laid before him he shall return to the branch of the General Court in which it originated a true copy of the portion so disapproved, together with his objections thereto in writing; such portion shall thereupon be subject to reconsideration and re-passage in the same manner and subject to the same requirements as a bill disapproved by the governor, and if so repassed, such portion shall be deemed to be reinstated in such bill and shall have the force of law as a part thereof."[16]

[16] It was stated by the committee in its explanatory report that "the amendment numbered seven gives the governor a very desirable power, which is provided for by the constitutions of a number of states. Instead of being confined to the two courses of signing a bill or returning it with his disapproval, this proposal would allow the governor a third alternative, he would be permitted to return a bill with recommendations for its amendment." This provision, it will be noticed, combines the principle of the selective or partial veto with the principle of the submission of specific amendments, found in somewhat the same form in the constitutions of Alabama, Virginia, and Australia. The states whose constitutions give the governor a right of partial veto now number thirty-seven, besides Porto Rico and the Philippines.

Mr. Quincy's plan concluded with an eighth article of amendment, which would regulate the succession to the governorship in case the offices of both the governor and lieutenant governor should become vacant.

But the Massachusetts Convention dealt with this well planned and consistent program in a manner which shows decisively that the people of that state are not yet willing to trust their governor with more power than he already possesses, either in respect to his control over subordinate officials or in respect to his influence upon the framing and enactment of the laws. The seventh item of the program, giving him authority to return bills with recommendations for their amendment (substantially as quoted above) was indeed adopted without much opposition; and the eighth, relating to the succession to the office of governor, received the approval of the Convention; and these two were submitted to the people as proposed amendments to the constitution and adopted at the election in November, 1918. But notwithstanding the fact that the entire plan had the unanimous support of the committee, all the other items or proposals were rejected by the Convention, in all instances by decisive majorities and in some by a vote of nearly four to one. The general ground of opposition seems to have been an ineradicable fear that the chief executive, if armed with a greater measure of power, might turn into a tyrant. The leaders of the opposition exhibited a state of mind which was very prevalent and very natural in 1780, but which is a little surprising in 1918. In the course of the debates one of the delegates said that governors already used the legislature for personal and party ends, and that the pending proposition would make the evil worse. Another declared that it would "make the governor more than ever the party boss." Another "thought the policy of the government should originate with the people. The legislature was more truly representative of the sentiment of the state than the governor." Still another declared his belief that "the proposed system would enable a governor to foist his views upon the people and reduce the legislature to a rubber stamp." Another expressed the view that these proposals "would make the governors either autocrats or nonentities," and urged the Convention "not to expose the state to the destruction of political liberty by a despot." This evoked applause. And the general attitude of distrust and fear was summed up in a declaration by one of the delegates that to give the governor power to appeal to the people for their approval of administrative measures which the legislature refused to pass "would give a demagogic governor opportunity to work irreparable harm to the interests of both capital and labor."

Similar considerations, it is probable, brought about the rejection of another very interesting proposal made to the Massachusetts Convention, to the effect that power should be granted to the Executive Council to issue orders relating to local, special, or private matters, which, unless annulled by the General Court, should have the force of law. An influential Boston newspaper commented favorably upon this proposition, in the following terms:

"The first great gain accruing from such an arrangement is obvious. It would relieve the General Court from a heavy burden of legislative detail. During recent years the annual ruck of bills affecting only a particular city or town, a single citizen, or some matter of minor import within any one of our hundred state boards and commissions, has outrun all patience. It crowds the legislative docket, it unduly prolongs the session, and, what is worst of all, it destroys the legislature's sense of proportion. The senate and house are neither left time to deal as they should with matters of large importance nor given a chance to see through the maze of their calendar to an estimate of what things truly deserve their attention. The acts and resolves of our General Court for the State of Massachusetts exceed in number each year the acts of the London Parliament for the whole British Empire. The explanation of this anomaly is that the Parliament has discovered the secret of reducing the bulk and the multiplicity of its legislation. It has conferred upon at least five of the cabinet ministers power to pass 'provisional orders' in many classes of matters, and to give these orders the effect of law unless and until, at the time when they come into Parliament in the form of one general act, any one of them may be stricken out or amended. The wisdom of such disposition seems almost self-evident. The only points for Massachusetts to solve are the questions, what exact application of the system should be made in this commonwealth, and to whom should the power of passing statutory orders be trusted? To this latter question the committee reporting on the subject to the Constitutional Convention finds the answer in the Executive Council. More and more frequently during recent years, the General Court, in a strenuous effort to relieve itself of some share of its manifold duties, has been delegating functions of a legislative character to the governor's council. Indeed, upon a complete study of the many matters so committed, all talk of abolishing the Council begins to appear very poorly advised. Far more natural would it be to certify and confirm the Council's new role by giving it the right to pass the proposed provisional orders. This is what the reporting committee suggests. As to the regulations which shall govern the grant, they are many and several.

They do not permit the Council to pass any order involving an expenditure of the commonwealth's funds unless from an appropriation already made. They provide that whenever an order fails to receive a unanimous vote of the Council's membership, together with the approval of the governor, it shall be left open to amendment or outright annullment by the General Court. The legislature's authority is thus preserved intact within all reasonable limits, and at the same time the legislature's promise of usefulness, with respect to all matters of major importance, is greatly increased, to say nothing of the new despatch and simplicity which the Council system would bring to pass in the conduct of local and state administration. The proposal here outlined is not of that commanding value which would inhere in some truly great constitutional move to enhance the powers of the executive branch in all matters of legislation, and thus to increase and determine the executive's responsibility to the people at large. But it is a soundly considered reform which may well be taken on its own merits."[17]

Whatever may be thought of the rest of the program, it is to be regretted that Massachusetts has not been willing to set an example in reforming the executive branch of the government by reducing the number of elective officers, or, rather, by making most of them subject to appointment by the governor, and by giving the governor a much greater power of direction, control, and removal over the whole system of administrative officials. It is the dissipation of executive power, the lack of co-ordination among the departments, and the lack of responsibility to a central authority which have reduced our state governments to a condition of inefficiency and mismanagement. Nominally the governor of a state is its chief executive. Actually he is nothing of the kind. Al-

[17] Boston *Evening Transcript*, August 5, 1918.

most exclusively he is a political officer, and the executive power is parceled out in fragments among a large number of elected administrative officers, heads of departments, chiefs of bureaus, boards, commissions, and superintendents of this, that, and the other, whose independence of the governor and of each other has resulted in an almost complete disintegration of the executive branch.

"American administrative law," says a recent writer on that subject, "has added to the famous trinity of Montesquieu a fourth department, viz., the administrative department, which is almost entirely independent of the chief executive, and which, so far as the central administration is concerned, is assigned to a number of officers not only independent of the governor but independent of each other."

In the first place, the movement by which, during the first half of the nineteenth century, the greater part of the chief administrative offices, as well as those of the counties and cities, were made elective by popular vote was a movement in the direction of democratizing the government, but it brought the inevitable penalty of decentralization. On this subject Professor Holcombe has well said:

"The direct popular election of the principal executive officers, at the same time that it rendered them more independent of the legislatures, also rendered them more independent of one another. The governor, secretary of state, treasurer, attorney general, and other central officers became supreme, each in his own department. They became severally and equally responsible to the people. In a word, the executive branch of the state governments became what is technically known as a plural executive. The direct popular election of subordinate and local administrative officers produced a similar effect. The sheriff, county clerk, county treasurer, prosecuting

attorney, and other similar officials became supreme,
each in his own department. They became severally and
equally responsible to the people. Thus the state executives were decentralized as well as disintegrated. . . .
Candidates for state and local administrative offices on
the same party ticket were bound to make common cause
with one another during the campaign. After election,
however, their community of interest centered around
the problem of re-election rather than around the work
of public administration. Party ties had their place in
purely political affairs, but except for the governor the
administrative officers had no legitimate connection with
affairs of that nature. State or county administrative
officers might form rings for their mutual political bene
fit, but they rarely formed rings for the benefit of the
public. Between state and local officials, party ties as
such were of even less use in promoting systematic and
efficient administrative action. . . . The disorganization
of state administration was in striking contrast to the
centralization and integration of party management."[18]

To undo all this and restore efficiency to the government, it would be necessary to give the governor not
only the power to appoint the members of his administrative staff and the heads of the various departments, but also to remove them from office, on a more
or less summary process, when such a step was deemed
necessary in the public interests. These powers are
vested in the President of the United States, who is
the real and not merely the nominal head of the whole
federal hierarchy. Such powers are considered absolutely indispensable in the case of the responsible head
of any important private or semi-public business. Is
the example of the United States unworthy of consideration? Is the result of the federal experiment dis-

[18] Arthur N. Holcombe, "State Government in the United
States," pp. 280, 282.

couraging? Is the conduct of the business of a commonwealth of less importance than that of a manufacturing enterprise?

"The framers of our Constitution," observes a former President, "had one essential feature of efficient government clearly in mind. They gave to the executive officer charged in law with the responsibility, and actually charged by the people with the responsibility, of carrying on the executive department of the government the power and means of meeting that responsibility. They vested in him complete power to appoint all the officers of the government who were subordinate to him, and upon whose political capacity and governmental discretion would depend the wise carrying out of his policies. They gave him the power of absolute removal, and they placed in his hands the control of the action of all those who took part in the discharge of the political duties of the executive department. They acted on a sound political principle, and it ought to be introduced into every field of governmental activity, into the states and into the cities. The plan under which a dozen state officers engaged in executing the laws are elected on one ticket and have no relation of subordination to the normal executive head, the governor, is as absurd as it can be. It is one of those anomalies in our political history, of which there are a number, which seem to refute the idea that we are an intelligent and clear-sighted people, because the system adopted is so utterly at variance with the teachings of experience. But we have had such governments—indeed most of our state governments are of this kind. They have not been as good governments as they might have been or as they ought to have been, and yet they have worked. The fact that they have worked may properly be taken as the most conclusive evidence of the political capacity of the American people through public opinion to maintain a fairly good government, and to get along somehow with what seems *a priori* to be an impossible system."[19]

[19] William H. Taft, "Our Chief Magistrate," p. 76.

But it is not only the heads of departments who should be subject to discipline and removal by the governor. To secure a really efficient and well articulated executive department, it would be necessary that this power should reach down to all of the officers, including those of the counties if not of the cities, who have to do with carrying the laws into effect. As experience is the best teacher, and a lesson from history is more impressive than any amount of abstract reasoning, we may be content to leave this part of the subject with the recital of the following anecdote, vouched for by a very high authority on constitutional government:

"Not very long ago a mob of unmasked men rescued a prisoner with whom they sympathized from the sheriff of a county in one of our states. The circumstances of the rescue made it very evident that the sheriff had made no serious attempt to prevent the rescue. He had had reason to expect it, and had provided no sufficient armed guard for his prisoner. The case was so flagrant that the governor of the state wrote the sheriff a sharp letter of reprimand, censuring him very justly for his neglect of duty. The sheriff replied in an open letter, in which he curtly bade the governor mind his own business. The sheriff was, he said, a servant of his county, responsible to its voters and not to the governor. And his impertinence was the law itself. The governor had no more authority over him than the youngest citizen. He was responsible only to the people of his own county, from whose ranks the mob had come which had taken his prisoner away from him. He could have been brought to book only by indictment and trial—indictment at the instance of a district attorney elected on the same ticket with himself, by a grand jury of men who had voted for him, and trial by a petit jury of his neighbors, whose sympathy with the rescue might be presumed from the circumstances."[20]

[20] Woodrow Wilson, "Constitutional Government in the United States" (1908), p. 204.

But further, if the regime of government by boards and commissions is to continue, it will be absolutely necessary for the proper integration of the state government, the harmonious working of its various organs, and the efficient conduct of its business, that these shall be brought more directly under the guidance and control of the governor. The boards and commissions alluded to are those which are vested with the state's authority and power of regulation over such matters as public education, the banks, the railroads, corporations in general, public utility companies in particular, insurance, charities, agriculture, the conservation and development of natural resources, game and fisheries, the public health, workmen's compensation or insurance, employment, labor statistics, and so on. It is rather amazing to read that, in Massachusetts,

"at present there are more than one hundred separate administrative agencies of the central government charged with the direct enforcement of law or with the supervision of the activities of local administrative authorities.[21] In Illinois, also, there are more than one hundred separate state offices, boards, and commissions, created by statute, in addition to those created by the constitution. Less than a fourth of those now in existence were created before 1870, and more than a third have been cre-

[21] But an amendment to the constitution of Massachusetts adopted in 1918 provides that, on or before January 1, 1921, "the executive and administrative work of the commonwealth shall be organized in not more than twenty departments, in one of which every executive and administrative office, board and commission, except those officers serving directly under the governor or the council, shall be placed. Such departments shall be under such supervision and regulation as the general court may from time to time prescribe by law."

ated since 1900. In New York there were in 1915 no less than 152 separate state administrative agencies. There are no other states in which the growth in the activities of the central government has produced so many separate administrative agencies as in New York, but there is no state where the organization of the administrative branch of the government retains its early nineteenth-century simplicity."[22]

In the government of the United States also we have witnessed the rise of commissions of vast importance and of even vaster powers. Speaking only of those which belong to normal times of peace and which were in existence before the war, take, for example, the Interstate Commerce Commission, the Federal Trade Commission, the Federal Reserve Board, the Federal Farm Loan Board, and the Federal Board for Vocational Education, and think of the almost immeasurable influence (not to say control) which is exercised over the industries, the agriculture, the transportation, and the financial resources of the country by the small number of men who constitute a majority of the members of the several boards named. But in the federal government the process has been one of centralization, not of disintegration; and however much the administrative authority of the government may appear to have been divided and apportioned, it must be remembered that all of these agencies are responsible to the one supreme executive authority, the President of the United States, at least to the extent implied in the fact that he exercises both the power of appointment and that of removal over their personnel.

[22] Arthur N. Holcombe, "State Government in the United States," pp. 286, 287.

But it is far otherwise in the state governments. So far as control is retained over the administrative agencies, it is vested in the legislative department, not the executive. On this point it has been correctly observed:

"The legislature often endows these boards or commissions with large powers, and while these powers may be modified or withdrawn by legislative action, so long as they are resident in the board it is practically free of executive control, as the power of removal is either denied the governor or so conditioned as to make its exercise most difficult if not impossible. Thus the legislative power is enlarged by the creation of certain administrative offices, still kept, so far as they are dependent, within legislative control. In the federal realm these boards have given added influence and administrative power to the executive, since they are usually placed under his direction and he has full power of removal as well as of appointment. The governor of the state is prevented from being in the same sense the administrative head of the state, partly by the fact that his power of appointment is more limited, all or nearly all the important executive and judicial officers being now elective, and partly by the other fact that the executive boards of his appointment are generally beyond his control."[23]

[23] Finley, "The American Executive," p. 180.

VIII

SUMMARY AND CONCLUSION

If we still retain the belief, so long an axiom of our political faith, that the preservation of liberty requires the separation of the powers of government; if we sincerely mean what we say when we speak of democracy as the ultimate achievement of the ages and as the universal order of a re-born world; and if, at the same time, we expect our governments to be vigorous and efficient—then we must profit by the lesson which recent experience very plainly points out, namely, that the successful working of government to the end of preserving liberty, realizing democracy, and functioning with sureness and strength, under our constitutional systems as we have them now, depends upon the due balancing of power as between the executive and legislative branches. If the former becomes the master of the latter, there is a gain in the energy and effectiveness of government. But it is at the expense of liberty, because the will and purpose of one man are, to the extent of that predominance, put in place of the collective will of the people as voiced through their representatives. If the legislative power absorbs more than its just share of control over the operations and the destinies of the state, we make a nearer approach to pure democracy. But it is a democracy which dissipates its energy and fumbles its tasks. We have seen the one event emerge into view as the result of forces and tendencies in our national government. We have seen that the other event may fairly be predicated of our state governments as they exist today. In both cases there has been a wide departure from the spirit and the plan upon which our institutions were conceived and set in motion. In neither case is the final result to be accepted as satisfactory or even tolerable. But to both aspects of the problem the best answer and the solution most to be desired are the same—to arrest the swing of the pendulum, to restore the lost equipoise.

In the states, it is true, the process of readjustment need not involve any further restraints upon the legislatures. Rather, the balance is to be re-established by raising the influence and authority of the governor, now sunk too low. The various plans for making him a real factor in legislation, and the leader of the state in its policies and in its work for the public welfare— in short, for re-investing him with powers actually commensurate with the responsibility which he assumes on taking office—have been sufficiently discussed in the preceding pages. Above all, however, the process of decentralization must be reversed. There must be a gathering up, a reconcentration, of those powers and functions which have been recklessly divided and subdivided and spread broadcast among a host of boards, commissions, and minor administrative officers; or, at the very least, there must be a co-ordination of the executive agencies of the state and a fair and reasonable subordination of the whole to the control of the chief magistrate. Only thus can efficiency, order, co-operation, and progress be assured.

In the nation's affairs, on the other hand, we have witnessed the decay of representative government, and the substitution for it of a presidential autocracy. The Constitution declares that "all legislative powers herein granted shall be vested in a Congress of the United States." But where is the legislative power now vested? The enacting clause of every act of Congress represents it as vested in "the Senate and House of Representatives in Congress assembled." Formally this is true, but formal enactment is one thing, inspiration and control are other things. The Constitution directs that the President "shall from time to time give to the Congress information of the state of the Union, and recommend to their consideration such measures as he shall judge necessary and expedient." But recommending that a measure should be considered and demanding that it shall be enacted are by no means identical steps. Yet it has come to pass that practically all measures of first-rate importance are now, wholly or in part, written in the White House or under its specific direction, or in the executive departments. They are then transmitted unofficially to some member of the Congress for introduction, and forced through the legislative mill by the strong pressure of the executive arm. The President has obtained virtually complete control of our foreign relations and of our domestic policies as well. From being the leader of his party he has become the leader of the nation. Instead of being the adviser of Congress, he is its governor. The executive, and not the legislature, has come to be regarded as the trustee of the public welfare.

The balance of power is dislocated. Its restoration should not be a matter of making a law or a legislative rule, still less of constitutional change. If presidents were content to play the part for which the Constitution has cast them, if legislators had a truer conception of their office and a larger measure of devotion to their trust, no ordinance would be necessary. With more self-restraint and greater respect for the fundamental principles of constitutional government on the one side, and with more courage and independence and a profounder sense of responsibility on the other side, the equilibrium of the Constitution would be regained, the ship of state would right itself.

But perhaps it is impossible to return to the order of an earlier day. Perhaps the processes of institutional evolution have swept us too far along the current of an irresistible stream. It may be that presidents, not necessarily or personally avid of power, have found themselves borne on the tide of forces which they did not originate and are powerless to control. It may be that it is politically impossible for a body comprising more than 500 members to contend successfully for mastery against the concentrated power of a single magistrate, their leader by force of circumstances, and whom, for a fixed term of years, they cannot overturn nor confine within any definition of his office other than that which he conceives for himself. Or it may be that the greater portion of our people are careless of constitutional theories and practices, that they are satisfied with the conduct of the nation's business as it is, and that they prefer presidential government to representative government be-

cause it "gets results." Or if they have no positive
preference, at least they acquiesce. If this be so, what
are we going to do about it? It is unlike Americans
to let affairs drift aimlessly—that is, beyond a certain
point. When a growth has become too heavy or too
unsightly, we seek the surgeon. When a political situation shocks our sense of order and good government,
we turn back our cuffs and set it right.

So then, first of all, let us have done with secret and
subterranean and underhand and unacknowledged
methods. Let us cast away hypocrisy and pretense,
and renounce makeshifts and evasions. Let us take
this whole matter out of the realm of hap-hazard and
apparel it with the respectable vestments of due process of law. Let us proceed like sober men, who think
the serious business of government demands frankness and truth and honor, and not like children play-
ing hide-and-seek. If we have outgrown the rules of
the game, let us make new rules. But let us play the
game openly, and not put up with shams.

For the whole matter and process of presidential
interference with the making of laws is a tissue of
pretense and camouflage. Dictation lurks under the
guise of "recommendation" and advice. We still solemnly pretend that "all legislative powers are vested
in a Congress of the United States." The presidential
steamroller is masked with flowers of rhetoric, of common counsel, of deference mingled with desire. And
it ill becomes a truth-loving people to endure such a
system. If it cannot be brought to an end, or if we
really wish it to continue, we can make its paths
straight, we can free it from all necessity for dissimu-

lation, we can let in the light of the sun upon it, we can, in short, candidly acknowledge it, establish it upon a basis of legality, give it frankness instead of stealth, honor in place of opprobrium.

No constitutional change will be necessary. It will not be a question of bringing within the Constitution something which it does not now permit. It is merely acknowledging the existence of something which it does not forbid. It only recognizes the fact that our conception of the purposes of the Constitution, in certain details, has changed, or that there has grown up a "usage of the Constitution" which lies partially outside its letter but is in no way contrary to its explicit prescriptions.

First let it be admitted that the President's constitutional power to recommend to Congress such measures of legislation as he may deem necessary and expedient fully empowers him to recommend the enactment of a bill, completely drafted, which he may transmit with his message. But let us, in the next place, be very clear that there is no one else in the official hierarchy who has this authority. As this is written there lies before my eyes a press clipping which recites that

"on the eve of his surrender of his portfolio as Secretary of the Treasury, Mr. McAdoo transmitted to one of the Democratic leaders in the Senate a recommendation that there be enacted a law authorizing the Secretary of the Treasury, under restrictions similar to those now prevailing, to continue to extend additional credits to foreign governments. This recommendation was accompanied by the draft of a proposed bill carrying the suggested authority."

Surely this needs no comment. Or rather, it is a sufficient comment in itself on the length to which executive interference with legislation has been carried. But nowhere in the Constitution are the heads of departments invested with authority to "recommend to the Congress such measures" as they "shall deem necessary and expedient." In law, that has been reserved for the President. Let it be so reserved in fact. Of course there is no reason why a cabinet minister should not be eminently qualified to draft a model law on a subject relating to his department. As between such a draftsman and the average member of Congress, the presumptions are all in favor of the former. But his function in legislation ends with the drafting of the bill. The function of recommendation belongs to the President alone. In other words, department bills or administration bills, by whomsoever drawn, should be sent to Congress only by the President and only with his explicit approval.

How and by whom shall they be received? It would be a simple matter for each house to provide by its rules for a "Committee on Presidential Bills."[1] All

[1] There is a precedent for the appointment of such a committee. At the opening of each session, each house appoints and sends a committee "to wait upon the President and to inform him that Congress is now in session and ready to receive any communications he may desire to make." And so also, just before the adjournment of Congress at the close of each session, it is the custom of the Senate and the House to appoint a committee "to wait upon the President and inquire whether he has any further communications to make to Congress." Therefore it would only be enlarging upon an established usage if a permanent committee in each house were appointed to re-

such projects of laws should be sent from the executive offices to the chairman of that committee in either the Senate or the House (or perhaps to both simultaneously) and sent openly and as a matter of usual and formal routine, and not by the devious hands of some unacknowledged agent. And they should be sent to no other person whomsoever. If an "administration bill" or one "known to have the approval of the President" were offered in either house, that house should refuse to receive it save at the hands of its proper committee. Or if that were too severe a measure to comport with senatorial courtesy, it should forthwith be referred to the Committee on Presidential Bills—and not without some deprecation of the irregularity in the manner of its introduction.

In the regular course it should be the duty of the chairman of that committee to present to the house every bill emanating from the President's office, and, with the consent of at least a majority of his colleagues on the committee, to move its reference to that one of the standing committees to which it appropriately belongs. This determination of jurisdiction over a bill is sometimes the subject of sharp wrangling in Congress. It is to minimize this possibility that the proposal is made that the motion for reference should be made by the committee, supporting its chairman as its spokesman. Indeed this is one of the reasons for hav-

ceive from the President all such communications as he might choose to make in the form of bills drafted in shape for enactment.

ing a committee of several members instead of a solitary though official mouthpiece for the executive. For the collective force of a respectable committee might very well prevail where the voice of an individual member (perhaps not the most influential in the house) would not rise above the din of contending claimants for control of the bill. And for the same reason provision should be made that something more than a mere majority should be required to change the destination of the bill as demanded by the committee.

But the work of the committee would not stop with the proper reference of the bill. It might be ordered in the rules of the houses that presidential bills should be reported out within a certain limited time and that they should have a privileged place upon the calendar. It would be the duty of the committee to see that this course was followed. It should be the guardian of the bill (save for its discussion in the standing committee) until its final passage or defeat. Of course freedom of amendment need be in no way restricted. And who would champion the bill on the floor? Perhaps the chairman of the Committee on Presidential Bills. But he might be hostile to it. Then it would easily find some other defender. Have we not seen a bill, favored by the administration, for a conscriptive military service law discountenanced by the chairman of the committee having it in charge, and taken up and defended and put through by another member, himself ranking with the opposing political party? The inquiry is pertinent whether the cabinet minister to whose department the bill relates (who perhaps wrote it himself) should be admitted to the floor to speak upon it. But if the conclusions we reached in an earlier chapter, where the whole subject of the participation of the cabinet in the proceedings of Congress was considered in detail, possess any validity, they show that the course here suggested would be unnecessary and far too dangerous an experiment to be entered upon without grave searching into its probable and ultimate consequences.

It will be said that such a system of dealing with administration bills as is here outlined would tend inevitably to vest in the executive a virtual monopoly of the initiative in legislation, and thus to superimpose the distinctive features of parliamentary government upon a system which is in no way adapted to it, because of the fixed tenure of the executive. Undoubtedly there is that danger. But it is not so formidable as it looks. For no immemorial usage has yet entirely quenched the independent spirit of the American legislator, however much circumstances may have bound his hands. Say what one will, there are still, and there always will be, senators and representatives who are not content to be mere rubber stamps, nor merely to register another's will. Somehow, and within whatever limits you set them, they will speak their minds and cast their ideas in the form of bills, and struggle courageously for their enactment. It is clear that the congressman's individual power, and even his collective power, is waning. It will not be extinguished, but it cannot be denied that it may decline to a still more feeble glimmer. But if that is the price that must be paid to set right the shams which we have too long endured, let us not haggle about it.

Via antiqua tutissima. These proposals are not put forward as an ideal solution of the problem of the relation of the executive authority to the legislative power, but only as a remedy for an admitted evil, if indeed no other measures of correction will avail. At least the solution would put us back upon a basis of honesty. It would enable us to play the game openly and aboveboard, with candor and self-respect, without disguise or circumlocution, like men who love the splendor of noon and shun the miasmatic mists of twilight.

POLITICS AND PEOPLE

The Ordeal of Self-Government in America

An Arno Press Collection

Allen, Robert S., editor. **Our Fair City.** 1947

Belmont, Perry. **Return to Secret Party Funds:** Value of Reed Committee. 1927

Berge, George W. **The Free Pass Bribery System:** Showing How the Railroads, Through the Free Pass Bribery System, Procure the Government Away from the People. 1905

Billington, Ray Allen. **The Origins of Nativism in the United States, 1800-1844.** 1933

Black, Henry Campbell. **The Relation of the Executive Power to Legislation.** 1919

Boothe, Viva Belle. **The Political Party as a Social Process.** 1923

Breen, Matthew P. **Thirty Years of New York Politics, Up-to-Date.** 1899

Brooks, Robert C. **Corruption in American Politics and Life.** 1910

Brown, George Rothwell. **The Leadership of Congress.** 1922

Bryan, William Jennings. **A Tale of Two Conventions:** Being an Account of the Republican and Democratic National Conventions of June, 1912. 1912

The Caucus System in American Politics. 1974

Childs, Harwood Lawrence. **Labor and Capital in National Politics.** 1930

Clapper, Raymond. **Racketeering in Washington.** 1933

Crawford, Kenneth G. **The Pressure Boys:** The Inside Story of Lobbying in America. 1939

Dallinger, Frederick W. **Nominations for Elective Office in the United States.** 1897

Dunn, Arthur Wallace. **Gridiron Nights:** Humorous and Satirical Views of Politics and Statesmen as Presented by the Famous Dining Club. 1915

Ervin, Spencer. **Henry Ford vs. Truman H. Newberry:** The Famous Senate Election Contest. A Study in American Politics, Legislation and Justice. 1935

Ewing, Cortez A.M. and Royden J. Dangerfield. **Documentary Source Book in American Government and Politics.** 1931

Ford, Henry Jones. **The Cost of Our National Government:** A Study in Political Pathology. 1910

Foulke, William Dudley. **Fighting the Spoilsmen:** Reminiscences of the Civil Service Reform Movement. 1919

Fuller, Hubert Bruce. **The Speakers of the House.** 1909

Griffith, Elmer C. **The Rise and Development of the Gerrymander.** 1907

Hadley, Arthur Twining. **The Relations Between Freedom and Responsibility in the Evolution of Democratic Government.** 1903

Hart, Albert Bushnell. **Practical Essays on American Government.** 1893

Holcombe, Arthur N. **The Political Parties of To-Day:** A Study in Republican and Democratic Politics. 1924

Hughes, Charles Evans. **Conditions of Progress in Democratic Government.** 1910

Kales, Albert M. **Unpopular Government in the United States.** 1914

Kent, Frank R. **The Great Game of Politics.** 1930

Lynch, Denis Tilden. **"Boss" Tweed:** The Story of a Grim Generation. 1927

McCabe, James D., Jr. (Edward Winslow Martin, pseud.) **Behind the Scenes in Washington.** 1873

Macy, Jesse. **Party Organization and Machinery.** 1912

Macy, Jesse. **Political Parties in the United States, 1846-1861.** 1900

Moley, Raymond. **Politics and Criminal Prosecution.** 1929

Munro, William Bennett. **The Invisible Government** and **Personality in Politics:** A Study of Three Types in American Public Life. 1928/1934 Two volumes in one.

Myers, Gustavus. **History of Public Franchises in New York City,** Boroughs of Manhattan and the Bronx. (Reprinted from **Municipal Affairs,** March 1900) 1900

Odegard, Peter H. and E. Allen Helms. **American Politics:** A Study in Political Dynamics. 1938

Orth, Samuel P. **Five American Politicians:** A Study in the Evolution of American Politics. 1906

Ostrogorski, M[oisei I.] **Democracy and the Party System in the United States:** A Study in Extra-Constitutional Government. 1910

Overacker, Louise. **Money in Elections.** 1932

Overacker, Louise. **The Presidential Primary.** 1926

The Party Battle. 1974

Peel, Roy V. and Thomas C. Donnelly. **The 1928 Campaign:** An Analysis. 1931

Pepper, George Wharton. **In the Senate** and **Family Quarrels:** The President, The Senate, The House. 1930/1931. Two volumes in one

Platt, Thomas Collier. **The Autobiography of Thomas Collier Platt.** Compiled and edited by Louis J. Lang. 1910

Roosevelt, Theodore. **Social Justice and Popular Rule:** Essays, Addresses, and Public Statements Relating to the Progressive Movement, 1910-1916 (*The Works of Theodore Roosevelt,* Memorial Edition, Volume XIX) 1925

Root, Elihu. **The Citizen's Part in Government** and **Experiments in Government and the Essentials of the Constitution.** 1907/1913. Two volumes in one

Rosten, Leo C. **The Washington Correspondents.** 1937

Salter, J[ohn] T[homas]. **Boss Rule:** Portraits in City Politics. 1935

Schattschneider, E[lmer] E[ric]. **Politics, Pressures and the Tariff:** A Study of Free Private Enterprise in Pressure Politics, as Shown in the 1929-1930 Revision of the Tariff. 1935

Smith, T[homas] V. and Robert A. Taft. **Foundations of Democracy:** A Series of Debates. 1939

The Spoils System in New York. 1974

Stead, W[illiam] T. **Satan's Invisible World Displayed,** Or, Despairing Democracy. A Study of Greater New York (The Review of Reviews Annual) 1898

Van Devander, Charles W. **The Big Bosses.** 1944

Wallis, J[ames] H. **The Politician:** His Habits, Outcries and Protective Coloring. 1935

Werner, M[orris] R. **Privileged Characters.** 1935

White, William Allen. **Politics:** The Citizen's Business. 1924

Wooddy, Carroll Hill. **The Case of Frank L. Smith:** A Study in Representative Government. 1931

Wooddy, Carroll Hill. **The Chicago Primary of 1926:** A Study in Election Methods. 1926